"Why are we so qui[...] [...] visions of God? How can believers' desires become one with those of their Maker? Matt Edwards not only addresses these questions with biblical clarity but leaves the reader with a burning desire to pursue a deeper and more meaningful relationship with God."

Leighton Flowers
Youth Evangelism Director
Baptist General Convention of Texas
Wylie, TX

"I have a strong, positive recollection of Matt Edwards during his student days at Howard Payne University, and thankfully, he hasn't changed much.

He was filled with youthful enthusiasm, fortified by bedrock faith and dogged determination.

In his book that dissects prayer from every direction, he remains deadest on the importance of prayer, illustrating with a litany of personal experiences how it has buoyed his life and ministry.

His work bathed in scripture is 'heart to heart'—from his to his reader's, reminding us time and again that God is infinitely bigger than anything we've seen, heard or done. Edwards' book reminds us that prayer remains our strongest linkage to him.

I thank God for Matt Edwards, who, time and again, has walked to the very edge of all the light he can see, with the courage of and childlike faith to take another step.

Dr. Don Newbury
Chancellor
Howard Payne University
Burleson, TX

"The book you are holding in your hand is not just another book. Rather it is the story of one man's journey of faith. I have been privileged to know this man and to witness much of what he shares in these pages. Matt Edwards knows the faithfulness of God, not simply in theory, but in the reality of a life lived.

Determined to be all that God asked of him, he remained stead-fast in this belief that God had a special plan for him and his family. It is recognized that God uses three primary means of growing our faith. He uses His word, He uses prayer and He uses adversity.

Matt is a man of the Word, a man of prayer and this book shares the valuable insight that will challenge your own prayer life. Most of us seek out the Word and desire to be people of prayer. But who looks for adversity? Matt Edwards stood his ground in the face of adversity, believing that it was God's will for his life.

You will be blessed and God will be honored as you read these pages."

Charles M. Roberts
Pastor, Denman Avenue Baptist Church
Lufkin, TX

Matt Edwards

Mark 4:23-24

BEHOLD THE
FAITHFULNESS
OF GOD

MATT EDWARDS

Belleville, Ontario, Canada

Library and Archives Canada Cataloguing in Publication

Edwards, Matt, 1966-

　　Behold the faithfulness of God / Matt Edwards.

ISBN 978-1-55452-323-8

　　1. Faith.　2. Christian life.　I. Title.

BV210.3.E39 2008　　　　　234'.23　C2008-905625-6

**For more information or
to order additional copies, please contact:**

Matt Edwards
P.O. Box 418, 401 Main St.
Paradise, TX 76073

Guardian Books is an imprint of *Essence Publishing,* a Christian Book Publisher dedicated to furthering the work of Christ through the written word. For more information, contact:

20 Hanna Court, Belleville, Ontario, Canada K8P 5J2
Phone: 1-800-238-6376 • Fax: (613) 962-3055
E-mail: info@essence-publishing.com
Web site: www.essence-publishing.com

Table of Contents

Acknowledgments

A BOOK LIKE THIS DOES NOT COME INTO BEING WITHOUT THE help and investment of several people. First, let me thank my faithful God who has tried me, stretched me, sustained me and strengthened me. It is because of Him and Him alone that I write.

I want to thank my wife Brenda and my boys for their willingness to sacrifice me from time to time to go away and write. Their sacrifice allowed me to complete this book that God has had simmering in my heart for so many years.

I also want to thank Charissa Fishbeck who painstakingly read through the manuscript, offered valuable insights and encouragements and used her gift of crafting words together to express and clarify my ideas to help me complete this project. Your labors are far more valuable than you know and I thank the Lord for allowing His lines to fall for me in the pleasant places of our partnership.

Thank you First Baptist Church Paradise. You have loved me, prayed for me, believed with me and together we are only just beginning to behold God's faithfulness together. May our journey together continue for years and decades to come. What a blessing you are to me and my family. I love you and thank God for the sacred privilege I have in being called your pastor.

Let me thank each one of you who have stood by me during the trials of this life. You have supported my family and stood with me in ministry through counsel, prayers and generous financial provision. God knows your names as do Brenda and I. We love you and thank God for each of you.

Lastly, I would like to thank Cindy Thompson, our project editor from Essence Publishing for being such a delight to work with and her diligent efforts in helping us be able to put the absolute very best book possible before the reading public. You and your team have gone above and beyond the call of duty.

CHAPTER 1

Why I Wrote This Book

THIS IS THE THIRD TIME I HAVE STARTED THIS BOOK. EACH time something has happened to either distract me or delay its completion. Once I actually did finish writing it but then lost the disk the manuscript was saved on. To this day I have no idea what happened to that disk. Another time I tried rewriting it, but the anointing to write was not there, so I stopped. Not long after that, God took my family through a crash course on prayer for eighteen months. I will be sharing more of that experience in this book. That crash course in the lessons of faith served as a time of research and preparation to start this book again and to finally complete it.

As I am writing this introduction, I have just recently taken a new ministry position as the pastor of FBC Paradise, Texas. For the first two and half months that I was here, I wrote nothing. Not an article, paragraph or even a sentence, other than sermon preparation. I busied myself with preaching, shepherding, and leading, but I did not write. I did not write any books in 2004, mainly because I was being so severely tested each day, and it took everything I had, and more, to cling to faith for my family. We lived day in and day out in survival mode, and it was all I could do to keep my head above the turbulent water of our tests. I had no desire or energy to write books. In 2005 I began writing messages for the No Compromise Ministries' monthly newsletters, mainly as an outlet for the lessons the Lord was teaching me, but I did not write any books.

Recently, while sitting alone in a room waiting for the start of a church meeting, I felt that deep-seated but neglected desire to write. I had at most twenty to thirty minutes before the start of that meeting, but I began to scribble on the legal pad I had brought with me. I had no idea that the penning of those words on that yellow legal pad was going to prove to be a life-altering encounter with God. It started out as meditation on some Scripture and quickly escalated into evidence of a clear command from the Lord. God reminded me that He had placed a call on my life to write articles and books, just as He has also placed calls on my life to preach and to pastor. I was rebuked for not fulfilling that call on my life, and as a result I have prayed for more anointing and for more inspiration, accompanied with the discipline to write not just articles but also books. I have several titles burning deep in me, like *Shepherd My Flock, Surviving the Storms of Life, The Bread in My House Is Stale, Climbing the Summit of God, Running Toward Risk, and Behold the Faithfulness of God.* I have much work ahead of me in the coming days to be faithful to this calling.

Writing books has not been easy for me. My motivation for writing has never been money or fame but the desire to obey the passion the Lord put in my heart as a child. I clearly remember Christmas of 1978—all I asked for was a typewriter. Not a football, a video game, or any other gift typical of a twelve-year-old boy living in the days before computers, but a *typewriter.* I wanted that typewriter because for as long as I can remember I really only wanted to do one thing—*write*. I dreamed about writing great books and even one day winning the Pulitzer Prize.

I carried that dream in my heart throughout my school years, but when I was a junior in high school, Jesus marvelously and radically saved me. Before long, God called *me,* of all people, to be a preacher. Off to Bible school I went, putting my dream of writing away and leaving it dormant for the next ten years. Even when I returned to writing after that ten-year stretch, I only dabbled at the activity I had once wanted to spend my life pursuing.

At some point during 1998, I felt and heard the call of God to write. That call resonated deep within me, and I was thrilled to discover that God actually wanted to use my childhood dream for His glory. I began writing little books and articles, self-publishing a few. I recall a group of college students staying up all night with me to bind a book titled *Swimming in the Bathtub* that I was giving away at a youth ministry conference. A few years later, some friends suggested I hold a book signing for two of my books in Lufkin, Texas, where I lived and ministered for over a decade. I set the date, organized stacks of books, brought my favorite pen and sat behind a table for the next three hours. It was one of the biggest failures I have ever suffered. I sold three books, and two of them were sympathy purchases made by the store owner. Those who entered the store walked right past me, never stopping at my table. It was humiliating.

After such rejection I really began to question my call to write. I had been met with closed door after closed door trying to get my books published, and the Lord shut every door financially for me to be able to print and publish any more of my own books through No Compromise Ministries.

I began musing to myself, *What is the point of writing books no one wants to read?* So for well over a year, I did not write any books. The desire was still there, but my doubt proved stronger than my desire.

Eventually, writing was pushed to the back burner. The last book I authored was written over six years ago, but I believed it to be the most anointed book I had written so far, and for five years I prayed to have that book published. Every door was shut. The desire to keep writing waned. I was inspired with several book titles, my list growing to over thirty potential books, but they were not followed with sentences, paragraphs, or chapters. I quit believing in my calling and was disobedient to the Lord. I did not sit down with pen or paper or at a computer other than to write those messages of the month for No Compromise Ministries.

But God met with me a few weeks ago, before that meeting at FBC Paradise, and I knew it was time to write again. This week, while seeking the Lord in prayer, I began asking God for anointing to write. You see, I am not interested in writing little books that are here today and gone tomorrow. I don't want to come up with the latest, greatest formula for how to improve your marriage, raise your children, or manage your money. I want to write books that are anointed by God and will stand the test of time.

Next, I prayed for discipline to be able to write and finish the task. Then I asked the Lord to show me the book He wanted to me to write. I sat back to listen, and the message reverberated in my soul immediately: "Write *Behold the Faithfulness of God.*"

I knew that this book would focus mainly on prayer and what God had taught me while taking my family through eighteen months of testing. Prior to that experience I thought I understood prayer pretty well, but what the Lord required of me during that time showed me what a novice I really was. For eighteen months the Lord required that my family live by extreme faith as He took away my steady salary from CentrePointe Community Church, where I served as pastor. Initially I tried to run to another church, but for a year and a half the Lord shut every door, thirty-two to be exact (I was officially turned down by thirty-two churches). God was firm in telling me to trust Him for provision and not to get a secular job. He was also firm in telling me that we should not communicate our needs to people or ask for help from any source but Him. For eighteen months my family lived from prayer to prayer, watching God provide all our food, make a way for us to continue living in our home, and show us His faithfulness in ways that were and continue to be astounding. God called me to live a life demonstrating that He answers prayers and encouraging people to trust Him with their lives and specific circumstances. When we had needs, we took them to God in prayer. We did not, and still do not, try to manipulate those answers to prayer by dropping little hints to people to help us. We believed then and are more convinced now that *God answers prayer and honors the faith of those who place their trust in Him*!

I was inspired and encouraged by reading books about the life of George Mueller, whom God called to live in similar fashion—not for eighteen months but for over sixty years. Mueller's testimonies were thrilling and incredibly challenging to me. He lived most of his life with simple childlike faith, trusting God for daily provision to feed thousands of orphans, without ever asking anyone other than the Father for money. He was able to behold the faithfulness of God thousands of times during his life and ministry.

Do I consider myself an expert on prayer? Absolutely not! I wrote this book for the glory of God, to give testimony to His faithfulness in honoring the principles of prayer that are laid out in Scripture, and to give personal testimonies of how those principles were proven in the Edwards' household.

This is by far the most ambitious book I have ever attempted to write and has only been completed because God's anointing enabled me to write every sentence. I only hope it provides the reader with encouragement to really live out the principles of prayer in daily life.

Let me conclude with the story of how this book was titled. Several years ago when I felt the Lord leading me to transition from a full-time traveling ministry back to the pastorate, we felt called to start a church. When I reported these plans to our No Compromise Ministries partners, the giving that supported our ministry dropped dramatically. There was a stretch of time when I had to honor preaching engagements that were already on the calendar, but I was not receiving a full salary from NCM. At the same time we were trying to start the church, which was nowhere near a point where they could offer us a salary of any kind. I knew we were headed for some lean times.

A dear friend phoned and asked me what I was going to do. I told him I would most likely get a secular job to make ends meet until the church could get on its feet financially. He called me again the next day and told me he had a dream about me the night before. He said, "God told me to tell you not to get a job but to behold the faithfulness of God." That was all he told me. It was interesting but confusing and troubling at the same time.

I spent the rest of the day and a good portion of the evening trying to figure out what that message really meant. The next day I called my friend and asked him to tell me more about the dream. He said he could not tell me the dream but reiterated that I was to behold the faithfulness of God. More frustration and confusion followed—could I really trust that my friend had heard from God?

I busied myself with work in my office the best I could for the rest of that day and the next few days. Later in the week, I received a phone call from my wife, Brenda, and immediately panicked. She was sobbing so hard I could barely make out anything she was saying. My first thought was that something had happened to one of the children. When Brenda was able to get herself together she blubbered, "———— [my friend] just sent us $5,000!"

I hurried home, and sure enough there was a check from his ministry for $5,000, with a short note. The note included Psalm 37:25, which says, *"I have been young and now I am old, Yet I have not seen the righteous forsaken Or his descendants begging bread."* The other thing written on the note was "Behold the Faithfulness of God."

Now, five years later, that story and title serve as the backdrop for this whole book. God loves it when His children take Him at His word and believe that nothing is impossible with Him. God loves to bring glory to His name by making a way where there seems to be no way. He delights in moving mountains, which are but pebbles in His hands.

How I pray that your life will be forever changed after reading this book! It has taken God years to prepare me to write it, and now the journey of faith continues as I dive into the faithfulness of God in response to prayer.

Father, I thank you for all You have taught me and will teach me in the future. I pray for these readers, asking You to open their hearts and renew their passion to be men and women of prayer. I ask You to pour the molten lava of truth from Your Word into their hearts to scorch and consume all the things that waste their time and are excuses for not cultivating a greater prayer life with You. I come with nothing to offer from my cup except what You pour into it. If You can take these pages and spread them over this globe, driving people to their knees in humility and expectation of beholding Your faithfulness in all of life, I lay them before You as a humble sacrifice. May none of our lives be the same as a result, for the glory of Your name. Amen.

CHAPTER 2

Behold the Faithfulness of God

For the LORD is good; His lovingkindness is ever-lasting And His faithfulness to all generations (Ps. 100:5).

How many people will toss and turn in bed tonight fretting over life and doubting the faithfulness of God? How many believers will doubt God's love during their nights of weeping and turmoil? How many will discard the Scriptures because their finite minds cannot wrap around the intentions of a sovereign God?

This verse from Psalms contains several things we need to learn in order to lay a firm foundation on which to build a life of prayer. Without these doctrines firmly planted in the soil of our souls and minds, it is unlikely that we will ever become people of intercession or faith.

The first doctrine laid out in this verse is simple: *the Lord is good*. I know this isn't the first time you've ever read or heard that idea, but have you ever really grasped what it means? It doesn't mean that He is good *some* of the time, or even that He does good things, but that His very nature *is* goodness. It means that everything He does, gives, and says is perfect and beneficial, because anything else would be contrary to His very nature. The word *good* can have several different meanings worth pondering—"beautiful, best, loving, pleasant, and precious." Each of these words holds a wealth of meaning as we meditate on the goodness of God. Let's look closer at a couple of them.

If we believe that God is good, we are also saying that He is beautiful and His ways are beautiful. This may be the hardest concept for some people to accept. It is all too easy to call to mind circumstances—in our own lives or in the lives of others—that turned out tragic and are therefore anything *but* beautiful. During the terrible time of Hurricane Katrina I read about some patients in a New Orleans nursing home who were abandoned as people fled the city. Dozens of those elderly residents drowned, helpless to save their own lives. Another example occurred as Hurricane Rita followed Katrina, when a man heard a tree fall in his yard and went out to investigate. While he was standing in his own yard, the wind toppled another tree, which fell on his neck, killing him instantly. Those two scenes are not beautiful but ugly and heartbreaking in nature. How can we stand firmly on the doctrine that God is good in the face of such devastation and tragedy?

In order to believe that God does answer prayer, we have to wrap our minds around the fact that God is *good* and *beautiful* and that His ways are beautiful. In order to do this, we must take the long view of sometimes painful circumstances, like the ones I have just mentioned. In the short view, it may appear that God is unkind, uncaring, and unloving, but changing our perspective often reveals God as the good God He is.

I *know* God is beautiful. How do I know? Just ask my friend Jeff, who pastors Southside Baptist Church in East Texas. After Hurricane Katrina, the members of Jeff's church housed and fed evacuees, and then they turned around and ministered to those forced to flee Hurricane Rita, even though Southside had also been hit hard and lost electricity for days. Thanks to the connections made during that time and the willingness of those people to witness in deeds as well as in words, over a dozen people were introduced to faith in Christ, even in the midst of a terrible crisis. God took the pain caused by those storms and created great beauty—the expansion of His kingdom—in churches all across the southeast.

In the long view, God is not only demonstrating His faithfulness but also reminding all of us that this world is not our home. We are simply pilgrims passing through. The problem is, it is far too easy to be absorbed in the routines of modern life. We work, build, buy, play—all while issues of eternity are pushed to the back burner. Every time we experience a 9-11 or Katrina, however, we are awakened out of our daydream and shocked back into reality. Life is fragile; life is difficult; and without a good and beautiful God to lean on in times of difficulty, we have no hope. We know that God's Word says in Psalm 46:1, *"God is our refuge and strength, A very present help in trouble,"* but do we believe it? Do we live it? Without the peace of God in our hearts and minds we worry and fret over things we have no control over, like storms, cancer, stock markets, etc. But His Word tells us,

> *Be anxious for nothing, but in everything by prayer and supplication with thanksgiving let your requests be made known to God. And the peace of God, which surpasses all comprehension, will guard your hearts and your minds in Christ Jesus* (Phil. 4:6-7).

Another variation on the word *good* in our text is the word *best*. Do you really believe that God wants the best for you? I have seen too many people settle for second best or decide for themselves what the "best" might be, and as a result marriages have failed or have been a train wreck from the very beginning. I have seen preachers jump at the first opportunity for a new ministry without waiting for the Lord's direction, causing years of misery for themselves, their families, and their churches. I am thankful that God has protected me from both of those common mistakes. Though it wasn't easy, God forced me to wait for the woman who was His absolute best choice to be my wife. When I met Brenda, there was a bonding of my heart to hers like in no other relationship I had ever experienced. More than fifteen years of marriage later, I can tell you I have no doubt that she is God's best for my life. Brenda is my true helpmeet, my partner in ministry, my best friend and confidante, and the one person with whom I treasure sharing my life. I am so thankful that God shut other doors and ended some other relationships that I was heavily invested in. When the time was right, He ushered Brenda into my life. That is the *goodness* of God.

When we determine to trust God and wait for His best, we are blessed. Often, we grow impatient and take matters into our own hands rather than allowing the goodness of God to manifest itself in our lives—and we experience untold pain and misery as a result. Our good God wants to give us His absolute best if we will trust Him for it in every situation in our lives. God and His ways are good; they are beautiful; they are best.

Now that we've established that the Lord is *good,* let's look at another aspect of His nature, listed in Psalm 100:5: "*His lovingkindness is everlasting.*" *Lovingkindness* may not be a word we use much in our day and age—so what does it mean? This verse is telling us that God's favor, mercy, and kindness in our lives never end. His mercies are new each morning (Lam. 3:22-23.) If every ocean were emptied and refilled with the tender mercies of our God freely bestowed on His children, the shores could not contain them all. Like the endless crashing of the waves on the beach are the mercies and kindness of our God bestowed on people through prayer. His lovingkindness is always there, always available; He is just waiting for us to ask.

This truth became very real to us when God answered a prayer for our family that many would consider frivolous. Our four boys—Taylor, Tanner, Tucker, and Turner—were scheduled to enjoy a four-day weekend from school, but we did not have a penny to our name. We had recently found a major miscalculation in our checkbook that drastically depleted our funds. It was nip and tuck all week long heading into the long weekend, so I went to the Father and asked for provision so we could have some fun with the boys during their holiday. I prayed for two days, and we received nothing.

On the third day of praying, the same day my boys were getting out of school, my secretary asked me if I knew I had a check. When I told her I had no idea what she was talking about, she handed me a check for $150 given for some preaching I had done two weeks earlier. I looked at that check and shouted, "Hallelujah!" Was the arrival of that check just coincidence, or was it another testimony in the life of my family to God's faithfulness? I absolutely believe God heard and honored my prayer to have some extra money to be able to entertain the boys. Was entertaining the boys an absolute necessity? No! Was that money a blessing from God in allowing me to bless my children by taking them out to eat and to a cornfield maze? Yes!

Let me give another illustration. This past July I preached at a youth camp near San Antonio, Texas, a couple of weeks after being called as the pastor of my current church. It was a good but grueling week, because one of the elderly deacons in our church passed away and I felt called to be back for the funeral. I spent a great deal of time driving that week, completing two round trips. The gas prices were brutal, and after returning for the funeral I literally did not have the money to fill my car up to make the five-hour trip back to camp. But while I was at the funeral, a member of the family gave me a card with enough money to buy gas to get back and forth. Coincidence, or another instance of the Father demonstrating His everlasting lovingkindness?

That wasn't the only example of God's love to come out of that trip. Due to my change to a new cellular service plan after that camp, the host church was unable to contact me for my address in order to send me a check. I left the camp with the understanding that the church office would mail the check, but days turned into weeks and weeks into a month and finally I resigned myself to forget about it. God would not release me to contact the church about the check but instructed me to trust Him, and not that church, for provision. I prayed several times during those weeks that God would remind someone at the church that the check had never been mailed, but finally I forgot the whole matter.

Because of the move we had recently made, our cell phone bill amounted to four times the normal monthly amount. We were once again forced to do the only thing we knew to do, which was to pray for God's provision. Our prayers went unanswered for a couple of weeks, but suddenly a miracle came. The church near San Antonio that had hosted the July camp found our address and sent a check.

Rather than the $200 to $300 I had expected, however, the church sent us $1,000! Once again God demonstrated His faithfulness and lovingkindness in a powerful and practical way, as He has done over and over again in my life. He has always come through—*always*! At times He has tested me to the last possible moment before the provision came, but God has always been on time.

I can tell you honestly that God has never failed us, not even once. Failing even one time would negate the aspect of His nature that is *faithful*. Look at the last part of Psalm 100:5: *"His faithfulness to all generations."* The word *faithfulness* can mean "truth, security, stability." The God who was faithful to Noah and his family on the ark is the same God who is faithful to us today. The God who saved me as a lost and insecure teenager, in response to the prayers of many, is the same God who answers the prayers of my children and will answer the prayers of my grandchildren.

There has never been a person who has drawn breath on this planet who can say with integrity that God was unfaithful to them. Every generation has, does, and will experience the faithfulness of God. With Him, our futures and families are secure. I am not suggesting that trials and sorrows will not come into our lives. In fact, I am saying just the opposite—we will *certainly* experience loss, pain, suffering, and obstacles. Our hope is in the fact that no matter what comes into our lives, how dark the night gets, or how the steep the mountain peak is, God will be faithful—secure and stable—in *all* of life's circumstances.

That is a fact that many people cannot grasp. Multitudes are blinded to God's faithfulness through a veil of tears as they watch loved ones suffer and die. How many empty bank accounts have left people bankrupt of faith as well? Chronic pain can cloud a person's judgment of God's faithfulness, but God *is* a firm foundation we can build our lives upon (Matt. 7:24-27). We can run to His Word and tenaciously cling to His promises.

I know how easy it is to be deceived by the enemy, our raw emotions, and circumstances that appear to be hopeless. However, we must not allow ourselves to be duped by them. God is never taken by surprise by anything we go through, and if we trust and wait long enough, He will show Himself to be a mighty champion on our behalf. You don't even have to believe me—just ask someone like Jairus, who was given back the daughter he was preparing to bury (Luke 8:41-56). Ask Elijah and the widow woman (1 Kings 17:9-24). Ask the woman with the issue of blood (Luke 8:43-48) and the demoniacs in the cemetery (Matthew 8:28-34). Ask the widows in my church; ask the broken and feeble-bodied preacher who preached for eighty years in our community before being called home to heaven. Every one of them experienced God's enduring faithfulness in seemingly hope-less circumstances. Because of these stories and because of the miracles God has done in my life and in the life of my family, I am encouraged to pray more, to trust longer, to believe harder, and to be slower to doubt, no matter how bad things look.

I am not writing this book because it seemed like a fun thing to do or even as the fulfillment of my childhood dream to be a writer. I have been mandated by God to put these things into print and to testify to His faithfulness in my life over and over again. Some of the miracles I have experienced in my own life have been hard to believe myself. I have tried to record most of them in my prayer journals so one day my children and others can read my eyewitness accounts of the faithfulness of God, which endures to all generations.

Let me close this chapter with one of those miracle stories. It goes all the way back to December of 2003, when CentrePointe Community Church had temporarily disbanded and the Edwards family was jobless and without a salary. I had been invited by a friend to fill the pulpit of his church in Jasper, Texas, since their pastor had resigned. The week prior to preaching in that church I took a prayer retreat and earnestly sought the Lord about what I was to do. Was I go out and get a secular job? Would God open a door for another ministry assignment quickly? His voice, though not audible, was very clear to me. "Do not get a secular job. Trust Me, and do not ask people for money. I am your provider." I had no idea what the Lord had in store for us in the months to come. I sincerely thought that the answer was right around the corner, that He would open a door for us to go pastor another church within the next few months. I can say now that I am glad the Lord did not show me on the front end of that adventure that I was about to endure eighteen months of severe testing and trials like I had never known before.

I went to fill the pulpit in Jasper, Texas, after that prayer retreat and preached the message the Lord put in my heart for the people of that church. I felt not only freedom but the power of God attending me that morning. After the service I was greeting the people when one man pulled me to the side and began talking to me about faith. We were involved in a lengthy discussion about trusting God when the man's son-in-law walked up and, saying almost nothing, shoved something into my shirt pocket. When we left the church later on, I looked into my pocket to see what had been put there and found a check for $500. Why would this man—whom I had never met before—do something like that? The simple answer is because God honors faith and is faithful to all generations. With that wordless gift, God was allowing me to behold His faithfulness.

With Christmas only two weeks away, it did not take long to spend that $500. Brenda and I prayed, asking the Lord for provision to be able to get Christmas presents for our young boys. The following week I received a phone call from a dear pastor friend who lived in East Texas at the time. He told me he needed to talk to me and wanted to come by my house. We made arrangements to meet later that afternoon.

When he arrived, we were all in the backyard watching the boys play. My friend handed me a Christmas card and wanted me to open it right then, so I opened the envelope and inside found a beautiful Christmas card. I read the sentiments on the front, and when I opened the card, five $100-bills fell into my lap. I was stunned and speechless. Tears welled up in Brenda's eyes as I just sat bewildered. My friend told me he had never done anything like that before, but the Lord had instructed him to give us that money. We talked a little longer, and then he left to keep some other appointments.

I called the boys to come and sit down on our back porch. Under that cloudless blue sky, I gave each of the three oldest boys a $100 bill to hold. I said, "Boys, do you remember how we prayed and asked Jesus for money? Don't you ever think that God does not hear or does not answer prayer. God heard our prayers, and God has done a miracle."

How many times have I had to remind myself of that same lesson? It is easy to doubt and to begin to entertain thoughts that God will not come through or that He is not trustworthy. But I don't care how things look in your life right now; if you continue trusting and waiting on the Lord, I guarantee that He will *show Himself faithful.* It is His nature, and therefore He has never before and never will be unfaithful. We can count on God. When the waters are rising and we think we are going to drown, God will rescue us. He will bring provision right on time. His hand of healing will come at the appointed hour. God will not forsake or abandon us in our time of need. Psalm 46:1 assures us of this truth: *"God is our refuge and strength, A very present help in trouble."*

Now that we have some fundamental truths about the nature of God engrained into our spiritual DNA, let us press on to learn more about His faithfulness through prayer.

Chapter 3

Secret Prayer

"When you pray, you are not to be like the hypocrites; for they love to stand and pray in the synagogues and on the street corners so that they may be seen by men. Truly I say to you, they have their reward in full. But you, when you pray, go into your inner room, close your door and pray to your Father who is in secret, and your Father who sees what is done in secret will reward you. And when you are praying, do not use meaningless repetition as the Gentiles do, for they suppose that they will be heard for their many words" (Matt. 6:5-7).

I once read an amusing story about the famous evangelist D. L. Moody. He was preaching a crusade somewhere when a certain gentleman in the congregation was asked to close in prayer. Proudly the man stood, began to pray, and kept going—rambling on and on and using every religious phrase he could call to mind. Finally, while the man was still "praying," Moody arose, stepped to the pulpit, and said, "Let's all turn to hymn number 342 and sing a little while so this brother can catch up on his praying." I can't tell you how many times I have wished for that kind of boldness,

which is an unfortunate indictment on our current understanding of the meaning of prayer.

Everyone would agree that prayer is an important com-
ponent to a healthy relationship with God, but most of us
put too little effort into prayer for the word *important* to be
associated with it at all. I have learned that if you really want
to be a man or woman of prayer you can be assured of three
things: prayer is *hard work,* it is *time consuming,* and it
requires *solitude.* These are three things that scare many
people away from cultivating lives of prayer. They do not like
the idea of working hard or spending vast amounts of time
in isolation like some monk.

I can relate to that fear. After being saved back in 1983,
I grew very little in my prayer life. I was not around many
people who knew how to intercede or to bask in the presence
of God for large amounts of time. I witnessed people praying
wordy prayers, but I do not remember ever being challenged
to cultivate a private prayer life of my own. I prayed privately,
but mostly for my desires, much like a child presenting a
Christmas list to Santa. At most, those private prayer sessions
would last ten minutes (okay, more like *five* minutes, with a
little Bible reading added on).

All of that was to change the summer after my senior
year in high school when the Lord called me to preach. God
opened a door for me to go to Howard Payne University on
a football scholarship, but I had no idea at the time that the
university offered a Bible degree. One day during football
practice I overheard someone talking about the Bible program, so I figured that since God had called me to preach, I
was to be a Bible major. Problem solved!

One of the requirements for participation in the Bible
degree plan was to be placed with an upper-class Bible stu-

dent for mentoring. My mentor was Richard Rozier, and we met a couple of times during the first few weeks of school, getting to know each other. One afternoon Richard invited me to join him for a prayer meeting with some other junior and senior Bible students. I accepted, although most of my prayers during that first year at Howard Payne were forced, awkward, and very short. My mind often drifted while I was praying, and I could not stay focused. Reading the Bible was much easier than learning how to pray. But I went with Richard anyway, and what I experienced that fall afternoon changed my prayer life forever. I listened as those students prayed, and I watched as they lay on the floor in humility before the Father—something I had never seen done before. The presence of God consumed that prayer room in the Phelps Bible Building in Brownwood, Texas, that day, and me along with it. I could not believe it when we finished and nearly two hours had passed. I knew I would never again be able to settle for quickly muttered wish lists or blessings over a meal. That day marked a huge change in my life, and I began hungering to learn how to pray more effectively.

Two other things really had an impact on my prayer life. I was introduced to an author named Leonard Ravenhill, and his books opened my eyes to a host of other praying men, like E. M. Bounds, Praying Hyde, and Reese Howells. The lives of these men inspired me to pray harder and work harder at it. I also read *The Hour That Changes the World,* by Dick Eastman, which outlined how a person could spend an entire hour a day praying. I thought this was impossible—it had never dawned on me that a person might actually sit down in private prayer and spend over an hour in that exercise. I read the book and tried the outline and, to my amazement, through concerted effort I prayed for an hour (watching my watch the whole time). I thought it was a monumental accomplishment, and I was feeling pretty good about myself until I read this statement in Ravenhill's book *Why Revival Tarries:*

> The prayer meeting is dead or dying. By our attitude to prayer we tell God that what was begun in the Spirit we can finish in the flesh. What church ever asks its candidating ministers what time they spend in prayer? Yet ministers who do not spend two hours a day in prayer are not worth a dime a dozen, degrees or no degrees.[1]

That little paragraph really shook me up and put me in a sort of bondage. For over a year I found myself looking at my watch or the clock every time I prayed to see how long it had been. As I look back, I understand what Mr. Ravenhill was saying but I see how that statement led me into several years of legalism. The unfortunate truth, however, is that many preachers *do* spend little to no time in sincere prayer. They may study for sermons, but few can be called true "prayer warriors"—those who wear out the carpets on their office floors because of time spent on their knees lifting up the needs and concerns of their church members and begging for the souls of the lost in the community. I can think of a few warriors like this off the top of my head, few of whom are still living today.

Ravenhill's sharp words in that paragraph and in the many other books he wrote cut me to the heart. I realized that if I was ever going to be of use to God, I was going to have to learn

---

[1] Leonard Ravenhill, *Why Revival Tarries* (Minneapolis: Bethany House Publishers, 1959), p. 18.

to pray. During these years, prayer became a passion for me. Sadly, it was pretty much all I ever read or preached about. I neglected many other great themes in Scripture while majoring on prayer. Even then, God began putting me through intense trial after intense trial to allow my faith to catch up with all my head knowledge. I had a lot to learn, and I hope you will allow me to share what God has shown me through the years as He helped me grow and shape my prayer life.

When You Pray: Reestablishing Priorities

In Jesus' discourse on prayer in Matthew 5, the first thing we must recognize is that Jesus used the phrase "*when you pray*," or a variation of that phrase, three times in three verses. His emphasis was bold and unavoidable—He never questioned the *importance* of prayer but expected that Christians *would* pray and make time for prayer. According to Jesus himself, prayer is to be a high priority in the life of every Christian. Read that statement again—prayer is to be a high priority in the life of *every* believer. No excuses.

I know some of you are saying right now, "You don't know my schedule. I get up before the sun comes up to get ready for work or get the kids ready for school. I am hustling all day long, and many times I have to work late. The kids are involved in soccer, baseball, football, dance, and Scouts, and then I have responsibilities in the community in addition to responsibilities at church. When do I have *time* to pray?"

To be blunt, that's not the right question. It shouldn't be "When do I have time to pray?" but "What is more important in my life and more worth investing my time in than prayer?" For many of us, that list is long. When *we* decide what our priorities should be, our priorities will be all wrong. By investing our time in so many other things to the neglect of our prayer life, we are saying that all of those things are much more important to us than praying is.

The truth is, none of us has any more time in a given day than another has. Twenty-four hours—that's all we get. Much of that time is chewed up with necessities like sleeping, eating, and working, and our leisure or free time is limited. Our calendars are filled with obligations most days and nights of the week, so we are choosy about how we invest our "free" time. We organize our priorities in this way: which of these activities will give me the greatest return on the time I spend? By this standard, prayer far too often fails to make the grade.

Think about the message we are sending with our lives. First, as Christians we are saying that we love God but we have no need to get to know Him better and little desire to communicate with Him. Can you imagine that mindset working in any other relationship? Picture me standing at the altar with Brenda, saying, "I do." After the wedding, I immediately change out of my tuxedo and get busy with the affairs of life—not even speaking to my new bride on our honeymoon. What if I neglect to come home for every meal she cooks for me or choose to eat on the run after tossing her a little "Thanks, I love you!"? Suppose on my day off, I take an hour to sing her praises and tell her how she is the apple of my eye and the love of my life, but on Monday I go right back to the same pattern—ignoring her, yet expecting her to take care of our house, our children, and my needs. Brenda would not stand for that, and neither would you in her position. But isn't that exactly what we do in our relationship with God? We neglect any sustained time with Him during the week and then show up at church and sing about how much we adore Him. We love God on Sunday mornings, and if we are really spiritual we might communicate or listen to Him on Wednesday nights and on Sunday nights. Other than that, we make very little time for the One we supposedly love.

I challenge you this week to keep track of the amount of time you spend with God in prayer, Scripture reading, and meditation. I am afraid we will all be ashamed. Jesus did not say in Matthew 5:16 "*if* you pray" but "*when* you pray." He expected that His children would make prayer a priority. When it is not, how can we ever really get to know God? Is it any wonder that we see passionless worship, mindless Scripture reading, and half-hearted service so much of the time? Part of prayer is communing with the Father and getting to know Him.

How many show up Sunday after Sunday and worship God from afar because they spent little time in the secret act of prayer? Ask yourself honestly—what real benefit do you receive from the other activities that take up your time? Take television. How many hours are wasted in front of the television? In what ways does television enhance your life? Hour upon hour is spent in front of that screen—at times flipping from channel to channel trying to find something worth watching. What about children's sports? Think of all the hours put in driving kids to practices and games. How many hot days have been spent at the ballpark only to come up on the losing end? How much money is wasted on sporting equipment that is later sold at a garage sale or passed down to some other kid when the equipment is outgrown or no longer needed?

I'm not saying that these things are bad in and of themselves. I just know firsthand that *nothing* in this world can bring true contentment and satisfaction to our parched souls like Jesus does. Jesus said in John 4:14, *"But whoever drinks of the water that I will give him shall never thirst; but the water that I will give him will become in him a well of water springing up to eternal life."* Drinking deeply of Jesus satisfies; therefore the more we drink of Him in prayer, the more contented and joyful our hearts will be. Jeremiah reinforced this point in Jeremiah 2:13 when he gave God's message to the nation of Israel: *"For My people have committed two evils: They have forsaken Me, The fountain of living waters, To hew for themselves cisterns, Broken cisterns That can hold no water."*

What return do you really get from spending your time in secret prayer? A life refreshed daily and satisfied in God. Nothing and no one else can do that. All other pursuits for pleasure will leave us empty-handed in the long run. When we pray and commune with the Father, we find the very things our souls thirst for: satisfaction, contentment, and purpose.

The question is not *if* you pray but *when* you pray. There's no way around it—you must reorder the priorities in your life to seek God *first*. For me, morning is best. Normally I get up before any of my family, and that is my time to seek the Father. If I am unable to get that secret prayer in at home, it will be the first thing I do in my office behind closed doors. There is no appointment on any given day that is more important than the one with God.

I have read many stories of prayer giants who awoke and prayed at 4:00 a.m. or prayed three or four hours a day. You are probably saying, "No way. Count me out. I agree that I need to pray more, but I don't have that kind of time." You know what? Don't beat yourself up—I don't have that kind of time either. But you do have time at lunch or early in the morning before anyone else gets out of bed. You can stay up

35

a little later at night to seek the heart of the Father. Whatever you do, make prayer a priority. Cultivating a strong prayer life will not happen accidentally but will require intentional and focused effort as you learn to reprioritize your time.

Do Not Pray to Be Noticed

Scores of prayers offered in public are uttered more for the approval of men than for God. You have heard these prayers—long, eloquent discourses filled with sentimental phrases, huge words, and even special messages that tickle the ears of people but repulse the heart of God. As D. L. Moody demonstrated at the beginning of this chapter, prayers like this are not to be respected.

If our motivation for praying is to gain the approval of people, we should be warned that human approval might very well be the only reward we will receive. Have you ever been talking to a spouse or a friend in a public place and felt awkward and guarded about what you said because you knew people could be listening? Praying in public can be the same. We feel awkward, and rather than just talking to the Father from the heart, we try to impress those around us by appearing more "spiritual."

Recently our church had a men's breakfast, and after the breakfast we spent some time in prayer. My heart was deeply grieved over how disconnected we men of the church were from each other. We attended the same church but barely knew each other's names. We ate together but could not talk on deep and meaningful levels. I found that fact tragically sad; it really hurt my heart, and my prayer that day reflected my sadness. Several of the men asked me afterward if I was all right, which was very uncomfortable for me. I found comfort, however, in knowing that I had prayed a prayer that honored God and reflected my heart at the time.

Don't fall into the trap of praying public prayers to please people. Don't think of phrases in advance so you can sound eloquent. Pray what is in your heart. The Father knows our hearts anyway, so we must be honest with Him even when praying in front of others. No matter what the circumstances, the motivation for praying should be to talk to God and secure answers to our petitions for the glory of His name. That's all the reward we need. I can't speak for you, but I *need* God to intervene in the mundane affairs of my life (Ps. 55:22). I *need* God to move the mountains that stand in my way of service (Mark 11:23-24). The approval of men cannot move mountains or heal my little boy when he is sick and vomiting. What you thought about my prayer during Bible study class does not bring peace that surpasses understanding (Phil. 4:6-7) or calm the storms in my life (Mark 4:35-41). We need *God's* approval for those things.

I actually heard a pastor at a pastors' prayer meeting refer God in the third person during his "prayer" (or, I should say, *sermon* meant for all of us to hear). Was he trying to reach the ear of God or impress a room filled with fellow pastors? Only God knows the true motivation of that man's heart that day. And to be honest, the temptation is there for all us. It is easy to fall into the trap of trying to impress people and to convince them that we are spiritually elevated. But the sad truth is, if earthly approval is the reward we seek, then that is all the reward we will get.

About five years ago I had a once-in-a-lifetime opportunity to hear one of my spiritual heroes preach. His name is John Piper, and he pastors the Bethlehem Baptist Church in Minneapolis, Minnesota. I flew to Minneapolis to meet a friend who was just returning from a six-month mission trip to China. We chose to meet in Minneapolis so we could go hear John Piper preach in his own church. It is hard for me to give an accurate account of the impact this man has had on my life and ministry. God has used his preaching at conferences, his sermon tapes and CDs, and of course his books (I have over twenty of them on my favorite-book shelf) to shape and mold my life and ministry—as a child of God first and as a pastor second.

Hearing this man of God preach in person in his own church was the thrill of a lifetime. I found myself sitting not ten feet away from one of my spiritual heroes. When the service ended, my friend wanted to meet Dr. Piper. Usually I am not into that kind of thing, but on this occasion I agreed. We waited in line for several minutes as Dr. Piper graciously ministered and talked to one person after another. I know he was tired because the service we had attended was the third worship service he had preached that morning.

Finally it was our turn, and we shook hands with a true giant of the pulpit. We talked for a few minutes, and then something welled up in me. I found myself asking this brilliant theologian, this world-renowned pastor, this best-selling author, if *I* could pray for *him*. At that moment I could have prayed a prayer to woo Dr. Piper and cause him to be really impressed with my spirituality. But that could never have happened, because John Piper would have seen right through all of that. Instead, I voiced an honest prayer from the heart:

"Father, thank you for John Piper. I ask you to give him endurance to keep preaching fresh sermons and writing books that impact the world. I ask you to give him strength and inspiration to keep preaching and keep writing. In Jesus' name, amen."

I will never forget his response to that prayer. He humbly kept his head bowed for a few seconds and quietly said over and over again, "What a gift! What a gift!"

The purpose of our prayers is to gain the ear, and the approval, of God and God alone. I pray that you will not fall into the trap of praying to win people's approval, for that is the only reward you will receive. So *when* you pray, offer sincere prayers to the God who listens and blesses your choice to commune with Him.

Go into Your Secret Room

Notice again that Jesus used the phrase *when you pray* at the beginning of verse 6 in our passage of Scripture. We are *expected* to make time to pray, but here comes another challenge—what about *where* we pray? Many people say they pray while doing other things, like watching television, listening to the radio, or doing other activities that distract us and compete for our attention. We are easily diverted if trying to pray without being isolated in a secret place.

Where do you do your best praying? Do you have a private place to meet with God in prayer day after day? I know a doctor who actually built a prayer closet in his house, a place where family members can get away from everything and everyone to seek God and lift up petitions. Not everyone has that luxury, but you can still have a secret place to meet with God. It might be a favorite chair in the living room, sitting by yourself at the dining room table, or maybe out on the back porch or under a shade tree. Maybe your secret place is at a desk in a bedroom or in your office.

Over the years I have had many secret places to meet with God but none more special than an office I had from 1998 to 2003, which had been the prayer room for the Denman Avenue Baptist Church for years. The room was abandoned after decades of use in favor of a different prayer room, so when I joined the staff that original prayer room became my office. I spent five wonderful years praying in that secluded little office, and it became my secret place to meet with the Father. I met with Him there at all hours of the day. At times I arose in the early morning hours to spend time with Him there, and at other times I prayed there late into the evenings when my soul was troubled. Often that room was stained with my tears and filled with fervent intercessions for the power of God to move in the East Texas region and beyond. Our first home was secured with prayers voiced in that office during my private devotions and in corporate prayer.

The presence of God lingered with me in that small office where I prayed and studied for messages delivered under the umbrella of No Compromise Ministries. It was a sad day when I was forced to move out, as the building was torn down to build a new sanctuary. I will never forget that secret place. What blessings and solace I received from the Lord in that private sanctuary!

Today my secret places are in a recliner near a lamp in our living room and in my office at the church. The walls of my office echo with fervent petitions for my family, my church, and my friends as well as for direction and kingdom expansion. Those are the places I have reserved to meet with God, and I cherish the time I spend with Him in those places.

Everyone needs a secret place to meet with the Father. Maybe all you have is a public place like the living room of your home, but you can still meet with Him in secret in the early morning or late evening hours when no one else is around. The *location* is not the most important thing—the fact that you have a place to pray in secret is what matters. There are things that take place in those hours of isolation with the Almighty that are life-transforming. Secret prayer is the lifeblood of any Christian, because during this time, God is able to give counsel, direction, rebuke, comfort, and exhortation and is able to dispense ministry assignments, remove burdens, move on behalf of other people, and bring soul satisfaction.

A couple of weeks ago I was preaching in Odessa, Texas, and my secret place of prayer for that week was a hotel room. That hotel room became my sanctuary as I prayed and marinated in Scripture for five days. While I was praying the Lord gave me three burdens and three specific commands for when I returned home. One of them was to go visit a widow from our church.

When I arrived back home, I went to see this widow. When I told her how the Lord had laid her on my heart to visit while I had been in Odessa, she began to weep. She spent the next several minutes telling me how she could not get over the grief of losing not just her husband but her best friend as well, and how she felt alone and that no one in the church really cared. How could I have known she needed the reassuring touch from God through the visit of her pastor? I could not have known it without sitting before the Father in secret with no distractions, where He was able to speak to me and impress this woman's need on my heart. I left her home grateful for God's leading to where ministry was desperately needed. If I had not spent time with the Father in secret and heard what He had to say to me, would that woman have received encouragement? Probably not.

I once heard a woman say that she spends her private time with the Lord while walking on her treadmill and listening to Christian music. Another woman builds her prayer time around a famous televangelist. However, most of us neglect secret prayer altogether, which flies in the face of what Jesus was teaching in this passage of Scripture as well as the example He gave in His own life. When Jesus needed to pray, what did He do? He withdrew from the crowds to be alone with His Father. *"But the news about Him was spreading even farther, and large crowds were gathering to hear Him and to be healed of their sicknesses. But Jesus Himself would often slip away to the wilderness and pray"* (Luke 5:15-16). *"It was at this time that He went off to the mountain to pray, and He spent the whole night in prayer to God"* (Luke 6:12). *"After He had sent the crowds away, He went up on the mountain by Himself to pray; and when it was evening, He was there alone"* (Matt. 14:23).

Since Jesus commanded us to pray in a secret place and set the example by often withdrawing from people to be alone in prayer, does it not stand to reason that we need a secret place too? Maybe you cannot find that secret place in the midst of the chaos of your home in the mornings or at night. Can you steal away to your office a little earlier and shut the door behind you to lock yourself up with the Lord? Can you eat lunch in a secluded place to be alone in prayer?

Recently I was given the privilege of preaching the funeral for a ninety-year-old man who had started to preach when he was only twelve. We affectionately called him "Brother Joe," and he preached the gospel for nearly *eighty years*. He never retired from his faith or from his call to preach and was actually scheduled to preach in our church the Sunday after he died. In fact, during my last visit with him in the hospital he reluctantly told me he did not think he was going to be able to keep that preaching engagement. He was a much-loved man and pastor in Wise County.

While I was finalizing some last-minute details for the funeral service, a man pulled me aside and told me that he had a word from the Lord for me. He emphasized that what he was about to tell me was not from him but from God, which really got my attention. He proclaimed the word of the Lord for me, and I stood there stunned. Through this man, God was reiterating a word that He had given to me in Scripture earlier that week.

Brother Joe's funeral was huge, and people were packed into our church. Though his family came back to the church after the graveside service to eat lunch, I was not hungry, at least not for food. My heart hungered to be alone with God and to meditate on the word that had been given to me earlier. When I was finally able to sneak away to the café down the road from FBC Paradise, I sat there nibbling on food but mostly pouring my heart out to God through the pages of my prayer journal. That café was a public place, but I felt safe and isolated in the presence of God. I don't know how long I was there, but I enjoyed a sweet season of secret prayer even in that public place. God used that time to mightily confirm the word my brother had given me earlier that day.

When I look back over my Christian life, most of the memorable moments have not occurred in public worship services or while preaching at different events. The life-transforming moments for me, day in and day out, have been those secret prayer meetings the Father and I have been maintaining for over twenty years now. They have been life-altering, to say the least, and they have been the foundation for developing a stronger prayer life.

When I stand in the pulpit and look out over my congregation, I have no way of knowing how much time those people spend during the week in secret prayer. I am afraid I might be discouraged if I really knew the truth about how little praying takes place—but God knows. He sees the one who drags himself or herself out of bed early to enjoy that sweet season alone with Him. God sees the one who brings knee-buckling burdens to Him in exchange for peace and help. God keeps record of the one who stays up late after everyone else has retired to bed just to have secret time with Him. That time does not go unnoticed. In fact, Jesus says the Father will *repay* us for that time spent in the secret room.

Did you catch that? That precious time spent in the secret room praying is not wasted but repaid. How? Work goes more efficiently. Energy is supernaturally increased. Peace replaces anxiety. Problems are solved. Solutions are discovered. All of this flows from time spent in prayer in secret.

I *want* to be repaid for praying—in fact, I'll just admit it. My motivations in prayer are few and simple. First, I want God to get the glory for His abundant ability to work on our behalf. Second, I pray in secret to be repaid with *answers*. I want God to answer my prayers. Third, I pray to get closer to God and to know Him more. Fourth, I pray for understanding of and insights into the Scriptures. I can honestly say that God has rewarded me abundantly in all of these areas over the years. My time spent in secret prayer is the best and most productive time of my day. As a matter of fact, before I sat down at this keyboard today to hammer out this chapter I prayed for both inspiration and anointing. The words and thoughts have flowed smoothly all day and the illustrations have come to mind easily, and I attribute all that to the time I spent in secret prayer earlier this morning.

I know we are all busy, but I would say we are too busy *not* to pray! We cannot afford to forsake this most sacred exercise of secret time in the prayer closet. To do so is to run vainly through life with our mortal strength, limited wisdom, and finite finances while attempting to live the supernatural Christian life. Look around you, and you will see the pathetic results of such living.

While praying earlier in the week I was reminded of two questions I have meditated on in the past: *What are you attempting in your life that will not be accomplished unless God intervenes? What is your church attempting that will not be accomplished unless God intervenes?* I found myself praying a weighty prayer for myself as a pastor and for our church. I prayed and asked the Lord for a certain number in attendance that would at least double the attendance of this church in her heyday and would more than triple our attendance today. In *my* strength it will never happen. My preaching and leadership are going to have minimal impact on their own, but if I stay in the secret room and beseech the Father to help, and if He chooses to repay me with a supernatural empowering and enabling, such attendance is possible.

O that God would move His Church to sprint to the secret place for prayer, there to be blessed by the open rewards and fruit of those intercessions! The kingdom will be advanced, the Church will be revived, hearts will be rekindled, and souls will be saved by the scores.

Avoid Meaningless Repetition

You know those people who pray endlessly in public. You can tell who they are when you hear the collective sighs and moans when they are called on to pray in a worship service.

That type of praying is specifically condemned. We suppose that the longer and more flowery the prayer, the more effective it is. This is not necessarily the case. Take for instance the prayer of Elijah on Mount Carmel while facing the 850 false prophets, found in 1 Kings 18:36-37:

> *"O LORD, God of Abraham, Isaac, and Israel, let it be known this day that thou art God in Israel, and that I am thy servant, and that I have done all these things at thy word. Answer me, O LORD, answer me, that this people may know that thou, O LORD, art God, and that thou hast turned their hearts back"* (RSV).

Depending on what translation you are using, this prayer is about sixty to sixty-five words long. I just read this prayer out loud, and it took me about twenty seconds. Yet the miraculous power displayed in response to this prayer was *huge*.

I am not trying to make a case for praying short prayers. I am trying to make the case that God is not honored when we offer lengthy petitions with meaningless repetitions or phrases. Sometimes I wonder if we are really *listening* to ourselves when we pray, because some of what we pray is contrary to what Scripture teaches. Let me give you several examples.

"Father, Be with Us"

You can hear this prayer on almost any Sunday in almost any church. Someone goes to the pulpit to pray, and you hear something like this: "Father, we ask You to be with us in Sunday school and in the worship service today." So what's wrong with that prayer? Isn't it noble and correct to want the presence of God in Bible studies and worship services? Of course! The problem is that Scripture already promises that God will be with us. *"Have I not commanded you? Be strong and courageous! Do not tremble or be dismayed, for the LORD your God is with you wherever you go"* (Josh. 1:9). God's promise to Joshua is valid for us today, that He will remain with us wherever we go, including church or Bible study. *"The LORD is the one who goes ahead of you; He will be with you He will not fail you or forsake you. Do not fear or be dismayed"* (Deut. 31:8). *"Make sure that your character is free from the love of money, being content with what you have; for He Himself has said, "I WILL NEVER DESERT YOU, NOR WILL I EVER FORSAKE YOU"* (Heb. 13:5). And the verse we hear most often in relation to church gatherings: *"For where two or three have gathered together in My name, I am there in their midst"* (Matt. 18:20).

Could it be more obvious? Praying for God to be with us is *vain repetition* because He has already assured us numerous times that He will never forsake us and that He will be with us every time two or three gather in His name. So why are we asking Him to do something He has already promised to do? Because we heard someone else use that phrase, thought it sounded "spiritual," and decided to use it too, without ever giving much thought to what we are actually asking of God.

A better prayer would be to ask God to help us to be *aware* of His presence and to be sensitive to His leadership. O that we could all become aware of His presence in every season of life—and especially when we pray!

"Forgive Us Our Many Sins"

How many times have you heard this phrase tacked onto the end of a prayer? Every time I hear it I wince. Why?

Because it is unbiblical. When this phrase is spoken in prayer it is in direct violation to the Word of God. *"If I regard wickedness in my heart, The Lord will not hear"* (Ps. 66:18). Scripture is plain that confession of sin needs to take place at the *beginning* of our prayer. We should start out with confession and repentance, and then God will hear our prayers. If we are ending our prayer with confession of sin, that is the point when the Lord begins to hear our petitions. Since He refuses to hear our prayers while we have sin in our hearts, we have only been mouthing some words that have ascended no further than the ceiling.

Another problem with this repetition is that we are using a blanket confession to cover specific sins. If I have sinned against my wife and I go to her and ask her forgiveness but cannot point out to her what specific thing I did wrong, my confession does not mean very much. You see, it doesn't cost us very much when we offer blanket confessions. In fact, it's much easier to just admit that we're sinful beings and move on. But sins are committed *individually*. We lie. We rebel. We gossip. We cheat. We neglect to pray. When I list those grievous sins one by one before the Lord, it bothers me and it is alarmingly easy to see my ugliness and my tendency to rebel against His commands. A blanket confession does not do that for me. *"If we confess our sins, He is faithful and righteous to forgive us our sins and to cleanse us from all unrighteousness"* (1 John 1:9). The word *confess* in this passage means to *agree* with God. We must come to the place where we can agree with what God says in His Word about sin. Read what Psalm 119:9-11 says:

> *How can a young man keep his way pure? By keeping it according to Your word. With all my heart I have*

sought You; Do not let me wander from Your com-
mandments. Your word I have treasured in my heart,
That I may not sin against You.

As we confess our sins individually and then go to God's
Word to see what He says about those sins, we are able to
resist sin and seek God. When we wander from His Word,
sin will not lag far behind. If we want to remain pure before
the Lord, we will stay in the Word.

I am thankful for a God who forgives and bestows grace
instead of justice on our behalf. The truth is, our sin offends
God. Our sin proved to be very costly for Him in the sacrifice of His Son. When we do not take sin seriously, I believe
that God is highly offended. I think that is the point of Paul's
statement in 1 Corinthians 11:27-30:

> *Therefore whoever eats the bread or drinks the cup of the*
> *Lord in an unworthy manner, shall be guilty of the*
> *body and the blood of the Lord. But a man must*
> *examine himself, and in so doing he is to eat of the*
> *bread and drink of the cup. For he who eats and drinks,*
> *eats and drinks judgment to himself if he does not*
> *judge the body rightly. For this reason many among you*
> *are weak and sick, and a number sleep.*

God will not stand for anyone cheapening the price Jesus
paid for our redemption. In essence, when we do not take sin
seriously and toss in one big confession in our prayer, that is
exactly what we are doing—cheapening the sacrifice of Christ.

At this point I could continue with other vain repetitions
we fall into while praying, like reminding God of His name
over and over again or praying vague prayers like "God bless
me" instead of offering specific requests, but we will deal
with these issues more extensively in another chapter.

The whole point of this entire Matthew passage is that you and I should pray sincere prayers and make secret time with God a priority without falling into the trap of offering vain repetitions or empty phrases that are contrary to God's Word to begin with. If we learn these lessons, we will be well on our way to beholding God's faithfulness.

CHAPTER 4

Prayer and Faith

Now faith is the assurance of things hoped for, the conviction of things not seen (Heb. 11:1).

You cannot divorce prayer from faith or faith from prayer—they are like two people who are married and have become one. Prayer without faith is nothing more than wishful thinking, and faith without prayer is wasted assurance and confidence in a power that is never activated.

If you want to learn how to pray, you must begin by strengthening your faith. Faith is just like a muscle; it gets stronger when it is used and weaker when neglected. If you want to have strong faith, you are going to have to *use* your faith and allow it to be tested under trials. This is the point where many people start abandoning ship, because they don't like being put in situations that test their faith. I admit I have done that myself many times. I have groaned and complained when being tested, but now I understand that every one of those experiences were opportunities for my faith to grow. Faith-testing trials might start out small, and then, as we are able to trust God in those situations and have confidence that He will hear and answer, we are able to move on to trust God for bigger things.

The first real test of faith I encountered occurred while I was attending Howard Payne University as a junior. I was called to serve as youth minister at a church about forty-five miles from Brownwood. Rochelle Baptist Church was not a large church by any stretch; twenty-five to thirty people attended Sunday school each week. The salary offered to me was only $25 a week, but I accepted their offer and began to work out the logistics. I did not have a car at the time, so we decided that Brenda and I would drive down in her little blue Nissan Pulsar so I could minister to those students. This routine worked for a while, but when Brenda went home for the summer to work, I was left stranded. I had enrolled in summer school, so I could live in the HPU dormitory, but I had no transportation and no way to get to my little flock of students at Rochelle Baptist Church. For the first month after Brenda's departure, I hitched rides with my pastor (who drove to Brownwood to work) and with other friends who were going in that direction on Sundays or Wednesdays.

In the meantime, I had become very close to the Munden family at Rochelle Baptist; in fact, I called Mr. and Mrs. Munden "Dad" and "Mom." The Mundens had two children in our youth group, Michelle and Cody. One day after a service the Mundens invited me to stay the night in the spare bedroom located off their garage. That room had its own sleeping area, bathroom and closet…it was perfect. For the next two years that little room was my home away from home.

Later, knowing that I didn't have a vehicle, the Mundens asked me if I would like to borrow an old car they had sitting in their barn. It had a huge dent in the side where a deer had hit it and no air conditioning, but it ran well. That car had very little that would appeal to a college student as far as the "cool" factor, but it was God's provision. I had prayed over and over again for a car, and the Lord came through by moving the Mundens to offer me the use of theirs.

The plan was that I would try to buy the car from the Munden family, but it soon became clear that, working as a youth minister and part-time for the campus maintenance department, I could not afford to pay them for it. But as I prepared to head home for Christmas that year, the Munden family invited me over, sat me down, and gave me a couple of Christmas gifts. The first gift I opened was a really nice shirt. Inside the second gift I found nothing but a piece of paper. At first I had no idea what it was, but as I lifted that piece of paper out of the box I realized that what I held in my hand was the deed to that car. The Mundens had *given* me the car outright. What an answer to prayer! I had been tempted to not serve that little church because of the low salary, lack of an office, and few students. Yet not only did the Lord triple that youth group in the two years I served there but He also increased my faith exponentially by showing His faithfulness in meeting my material needs.

What if I had looked at the small salary, the undersized congregation, the forty-five miles that separated Rochelle from Brownwood, and my lack of transportation and had refused to accept that position? I would have missed out on great faith training. How else could I have known the blessing of a car provided by God while serving that church? How could I have foreseen the incredible relationship I was going to build with the Munden family? How could I have known how many of those students' lives would be changed forever because of God's faithfulness during those two years?

To become powerful prayer warriors we must have strong faith, and to build strong faith we must be tested.

God will put us in situations that stretch our trust and confidence in Him. These times are not comfortable, but if we know up front that these experiences are part of faith-building, then we can endure, grow stronger, and move forward to trust God for bigger things.

About a year after the Mundens gave me my car, I entered my last semester at Howard Payne University. To my surprise, people began asking me what I was going to do after I graduated. I didn't really have any detailed plans for "after college"—I had assumed I would continue serving that little church and working in the maintenance department on the Howard Payne University campus. At that point God had not given me any clear direction about His plans for my future, so I was content to stay where I was and wait on Him. After my graduation (and a great deal of prayer), the Lord spoke to me in the middle of the summer, and I felt called to move to Fort Worth to enroll in Southwestern Baptist Theological Seminary. Please understand: I had no money to move. No money for tuition. No place to live. No job. The two things I *did* have were confidence in God and the assurance that He had called me to move to Fort Worth to enroll in seminary. I remember packing all of my belongings into the miracle car one August day and driving to Fort Worth, praying most of the way. In a matter of days I had a furnished duplex apartment to live in, a job, and my first year of tuition, which God provided through a person who wanted to remain anonymous. God made a way where there seemed to be no way. Once again the muscles of my faith had been put under a great strain, and they grew.

Hebrews 11:1 says, *"Faith is the assurance of things hoped for."* The word *assurance* can be translated "confidence."[2] In

---

[2] *Bible Soft PC Study Bible version 4.20* (1988-2004).

order to have genuine faith, we must have confidence in God and His Word. The word *confidence* is defined as a "state of feeling sure; assurance." I packed my belongings into that car and took off, just naive enough to believe that if God called me to do something, I could trust Him—that was the confidence I had in Him. Then I got to watch Him give me a job, a place to live, and a year's tuition, all in response to confident prayer. My confidence was in the Lord to make a way for me even though there seemed to be no way, just as He did when the entire nation of Israel crossed through the middle of the Red Sea on dry ground (Exod. 14).

I am not suggesting that you pack all your belongings in a car and take off on a whim to some place you sense Him leading you to. Yet if you truly believe He has called you to do just that, why not trust Him? If we would abandon ourselves to Him and follow Him no matter what, we would see powerful miracles, but most of us are content to sit on the sidelines and watch the miracles happen for others.

We demonstrate faith when we live and act like what we have been praying for is a reality *before* it ever becomes a reality. In faith, you must plunge headfirst into the darkness of uncertainty with no guarantees other than the knowledge that you have the call of God and the Word of God to do so. The more you do this, the more your confidence in God grows. The less you do this, the more your faith shrivels into doubt and unbelief. And make no mistake, you *will* be tested. If you are going to behold God's faithfulness, you are going to be put in situations where the Lord says, "Trust Me. I have everything under control." To the naked eye the situation may appear impossible, but if you want to see God's power, you will choose to believe Him.

A couple of years ago I faced such a test—or actually, a

single day full of tests—and was tempted to back away. One day during the eighteen months that my family was living without a guaranteed salary, I had a lunch appointment scheduled in Palestine, Texas, with one of the board members of No Compromise Ministries. Finances could not have been tighter for us; I had just enough gas in the car that morning to get to Palestine but not a penny in my pocket for meals or other expenses. I came very close to just cancelling the whole trip, but God had called me to trust Him, and so I decided to keep my appointments and let God do the rest. I prayed all through that lunch that my friend would offer to pay, and I was grateful when he did. After lunch I left Palestine and set off for my next appointment in Tyler, Texas, with a ministry friend. I prayed most of the way to Tyler, asking God for enough gas to get there and to make the 100-mile trip back to Hudson, where we were living at the time. Once again God gave me a courtside seat to behold His faithfulness; He prompted that ministry friend to give me a $100 bill without my ever saying a word about my need. I had a need, I had confidence in God to meet that need, and He came through as He has done time and time again. My faith was both encouraged and strengthened through that test.

There are times when we have to put our money—or lack of money—where our mouth is. One of the toughest times is when we are holding the offering plate in one hand and searching through our wallet or purse with the other hand, knowing that if we give a full tithe we will not have money to make it to the end of the month. *That* is when we have to have confidence that since God promised to be our provider (Phil. 4:19; Ps. 50:15), He will honor His promise.

Praying Specifically

Hebrews 11:1 exhorts us to not only have confidence and assurance in God but also pray specifically: *"Now faith is the assurance of things hoped for, the conviction of things not seen."* What are "things"? In the Greek language one of the meanings for the word *things* is "an object."[3] When we are confidently asking and trusting God for something, that object is specific. When we pray specifically, God gets more glory when our prayers are answered specifically.

Let me illustrate: about halfway through our eighteen-month crash course in learning to trust God for everything, I was invited to preach to a group of teenagers in San Angelo, Texas. I loaded up my Jeep Grand Cherokee, which was a miracle in itself that I had prayed for and was given several years earlier. It was a great vehicle, and I put well over 100,000 miles on it traveling to preach at revivals and youth camps. By this time, that Jeep had 198,000 miles on it, but I made the six-hour trip to San Angelo and preached to those students, which ended up being a wonderful time of ministry. As I made my way back home the following morning, I was enjoying some communion with God, just driving in silence down I-20 at about seventy miles per hour. Suddenly I began hearing a strange noise. I pulled over and investigated, only to find that it was my trusty old Jeep making that noise, and I had no idea what the problem was or how to solve it. I immediately began calling some of my friends who had much more mechanical expertise than I did, and according to them the diagnosis was not good. I was stranded about fifteen miles outside of Weatherford, Texas. I made some phone calls (thank the Lord for cell

---

[3] *Bible Soft PC Study Bible version 4.20* (1988-2004).

phones!) and arranged to be picked up, and a few days later a friend and I drove back to the Jeep to load it on a flatbed trailer and haul it back home, where it sat in my driveway for several months until we sold it cheaply.

When I discovered that the damage to the Jeep was quite extensive, I felt a peace in my heart that the Lord would provide another vehicle, just as He had provided the Jeep. I began praying very specifically, not just for another vehicle but for certain specific things about the vehicle I was asking the Lord to provide.

For instance, over the previous two years I had been driving the Jeep without an air conditioner. I will never forget trips I made in that Jeep to Arkansas to preach at a youth camp in June and to Odessa, San Antonio, and Beaumont in the sweltering Texas summer heat. In addition, my tape player had broken, leaving me unable to listen to sermon tapes of my beloved favorite preachers. The antenna had been knocked off while I was driving back from a youth camp, so I could not get much radio reception, and my efforts to put in a CD player that I had been given were not successful. I had spent the last two years driving in silence.

So when I began praying for a new vehicle, I prayed for a four-door truck with air conditioning, with a CD player *and* a cassette player so I could listen to messages while traveling. One month of praying turned into two. Two into six. Six into eight. Finally, in the ninth month of praying for a car, we had the money to go car shopping. I looked at several vehicles in the lot before I noticed a four-door silver Ford Explorer. It had only 23,000 miles on it, and the price was well below anything I thought they might be asking for it. I bought that truck and was able to pay it off quickly, and it was that very truck that I drove to Palestine, Texas, where I am preaching at a youth revival this week and enjoying a prayer and writing retreat for the next four days. And thanks to the sound system in the truck that God provided, I listened to sermon tapes the whole way here. God blessed me with the exact type of vehicle I had asked for.

Many would say this is "name it and claim it" theology, but I just say I followed Hebrews 11:1 and God honored my faith by giving me exactly what I had trusted Him to give. *He* gets the glory for it—not me or any prayers I prayed. I have already given God much glory for that vehicle, and this book is just another way to exalt God and allow you to behold His faithfulness, as I have been privileged to do on numerous occasions.

CHAPTER 5 —————————————

Mountain-Moving Prayer

—————

"Truly I say to you, whoever says to this mountain, 'Be taken up and cast into the sea,' and does not doubt in his heart, but believes that what he says is going to happen, it will be granted him. Therefore I say to you, all things for which you pray and ask, believe that you have received them, and they will be granted you" (Mark 11:23-24).

I love this passage of Scripture. There is so much truth packed in it to help us learn how to pray more effectively and to believe God for more. Before you read this chapter I would like you to identify the mountains that are looming large in front of you today: Is it the need for a job? A spouse? A car? A house? The healing of an illness? The reconciliation of a marriage or some other relationship? The salvation of a loved one? The realization of a ministry dream?

Regardless of what mountains are standing in your way right this moment, God can conquer all. Do you really believe that? Can prayer really make a difference? Absolutely.

"Whoever Says to This Mountain, 'Be Taken Up...'"

I have spent a great deal of time reading about the lives of prayer warriors: people throughout history who shook up the world with simple faith and trust in God to move mountains; men like George Mueller, who housed, clothed, and fed thousands of orphans without ever asking people for money but rather making his requests known to God. Over and over again Mueller and his co-laborers were tested.

For instance, one morning a female worker came out of the orphanage and told Mueller the day had finally come when they had no food to feed the orphans. She was panicking and did not know what to do, since the breakfast hour was fast approaching. Mueller confidently told the woman to follow the normal procedure, having the children gather at the table and stand behind their chairs, despite there being no food on the table. So plates were set and glasses were put out, and at the appointed hour the children stood behind their chairs...and Mueller began to pray for God's provision. While he was praying, someone knocked on the door. It was the milk delivery man, whose wagon wheel had broken *right in front of the orphanage*. The milk man told Mueller and the astonished orphanage workers that since he could not get the wheel repaired before the milk would spoil, he wanted to donate the milk to the orphanage.

Not long after the milk had been hauled in and each glass had been filled, there was another knock at the door. This time it was a baker, who commented that the Lord had awoken him early that morning and instructed him to bake bread for the orphans. Through these miraculous provisions, each child at the orphanage was given milk and bread that morning, and by lunchtime enough money had arrived to buy provisions for the rest of the meals that day.

Mueller faced a huge mountain that day, but he was undaunted and saw his mountain move—one loaf of bread and glass of milk at a time.[4] I could write similar stories from the life of John Hyde, a missionary to India. He believed that God would allow him to see one soul saved each day. By the end of a year God had exceeded Hyde's request. Before long Hyde decided to ask for *four* souls to be won to Christ daily through his ministry. Hyde spent every day either praying or witnessing, and by the end of that year God had indeed reached and exceeded Hyde's goal.

What about the prayer life of Hudson Taylor? Amy Carmichael? E. M. Bounds? Reese Howells? Andrew Murray? Watchman Nee? I could go on and on, sharing the remarkable stories of God's provision and the mountains moved in the lives of these prayer giants.

Let's read that verse again: *"Truly I say to you, whoever says to this mountain..."* We have come to believe that the aforementioned men and women were special, set apart, talented, or endowed with something extraordinary from God. But it isn't the people themselves who were special; they were simply men and women who knew the precious promises of God in Scripture and who had undaunted faith. There were times when each of them faced huge mountains, and yet they beheld the faithfulness of God in their circumstances. They asked, confidently believed, and saw miracle after miracle in response to their prayers.

---

[4] Janet & Geoff Benge, *George Mueller: The Guardian of Bristol's Orphans* (YWAM Publishing, Seattle, WA 1999,) p 166, 167.

You and I have the same opportunities they did, and we have the same promises of God that were given to the saints of old. Our Bibles say the same things theirs did. God makes increased faith available to us as He did for them. So why do we live in an age of miracle famine? Read what James says:

Elijah was a man with a nature like ours, and he prayed earnestly that it would not rain, and it did not rain on the earth for three years and six months. Then he prayed again, and the sky poured rain and the earth produced its fruit (Jas. 5:17-18).

Elijah was just a man—flesh and blood. He determined to believe God and to pray with confidence, and God did the rest. And the same God who has worked on my behalf—in all the situations I have mentioned and many more to come—works on your behalf just as faithfully. *He* is the one who moves mountains and turns impossibilities into possibilities. It is God who makes mountains majestically bow in His presence and be removed, and the more we see it, the more we believe it. We must always be careful at this point, however, not to boast in *our* prayers and *our* confidence and *our* perseverance as if it were through our efforts that mountains move. God does the moving; we just believe and ask Him for it.

On the other end of the spectrum, if you doubt your ability to be used mightily of God by moving mountains with your prayers, you are saying more about your lack of belief in God than in yourself. Of course you can't do it, but God can. You and I cannot do anything of kingdom significance apart from Christ working in us (John 15:5). Our faith may be weak, but God helps our unbelief (Mark 9:24). We are tempted to give up, but God plants the burden so deep in our hearts that we cannot let go without God's blessing (Gen. 32:26). God wills us to be mighty mountain-moving prayer soldiers who refuse to be denied until the victory has been won. God can use *anyone* to move mountains with the weapons of Scripture, fearless faith, and tenacity. *Anyone!* That includes you, and surprisingly enough, it also includes me.

When God put the call on my life to establish No Compromise Ministries and to leave pastoral ministry for a time of healing and strengthening of my faith, it was a frightening step to take. Not only was God leading me to give up my steady salary as a pastor, but I knew that this step meant we would have to move out of the Burke Baptist Church parsonage we had resided in for the previous five years. Brenda and I did not have money to buy a house at the time, and we had no income to rent a house either. It was a blind leap of faith, and the issues of salary and housing were huge mountains that stood in the way. We had no choice but to trust God.

Brenda and I wrestled with the Lord for some time over this situation. I felt as if I was on the edge of the cliff peering over, and all I could see was darkness below with no bottom in sight. I sought the counsel of my pastor and other preacher friends and seemed to get the same message from each of them: Trust God and *leap*.

I finally submitted to God's call right before doing a weekend youth event in my home church. There I met a businessman, in whose home I stayed throughout the weekend. During that time, we had several opportunities to talk about what God was doing in our lives, and I cast my vision for No Compromise Ministries before him, not realizing that God was at work in those casual conversations.

At long last, I mustered up the courage to resign as pastor of Burke Baptist Church. The pastor of my home church graciously offered me an office at that facility to use as I launched No Compromise Ministries. A few days after taking that leap of faith, I received a phone call from my pastor that powerfully demonstrated the power of God in response to prayer. He told me that the businessman I had chatted with weeks earlier about No Compromise Ministries had given a gift of $6,000 to guarantee me a $1,000 a month salary for the first six months of my ministry. My pastor went on to tell me that he had remembered that the mission church they were supporting had a parsonage, and he offered it to me to live in, rent-free, for a year.

Two enormous mountains. An ordinary simpleton like me praying and asking God to move those mountains. And one awesome God, coming through like only He can.

And Does Not Doubt...

Doubt is to prayer as water is to fire. When accompanied by doubt, prayer becomes little more than a wish list. Little children have more confidence in Santa Claus to give them the desires of their hearts than many Christians have in God to answer prayer.

There are naysayers and doomsday prophets all around us. There is no shortage of people in our lives to tell us that the mountains standing in our way have been there too long and are too large to ever be moved or overcome. They laugh at our childlike faith. They increase confusion and sow doubt where faith is so desperately needed.

Doubt hinders prayer. The word *doubt* can mean "to hesitate, stagger, waver, withdraw from, oppose." We must confidently trust God to come through, without the slightest bit of hesitation or wavering in our confidence. When God calls us to believe Him, we must not either withdraw in unbelief or oppose His promises. Look at this example from Scripture:

> *Jesus went out from there and came into His home-town; and His disciples followed Him. When the Sabbath came, He began to teach in the synagogue; and the many listeners were astonished, saying, "Where did this man get these things, and what is this wisdom given to Him, and such miracles as these performed by His hands? "Is not this the carpenter, the son of Mary, and brother of James and Joses and Judas and Simon? Are not His sisters here with us?" And they took offense at Him. Jesus said to them, "A prophet is not without honor except in his hometown and among his own relatives and in his own household." And He could do no miracle there except that He laid His hands on a few sick people and healed them. And He wondered at their unbelief* (Mark 6:1-6).

Even Jesus identified others' unbelief or doubt as a hindrance to His ability to do mighty works. Here is a terrifying thought—what does our doubt hinder Him from doing in our churches and communities? So little of our praying is fueled by the fire of faith; rather, it's drowned in the waters of doubt. Our prayer meetings and prayer lists often resemble wish meetings and wish lists. May we not be a people who doubt God and withdraw from the mountains in our path! May we march forward with determination and confidence in the power of our God.

I am reminded of a story in the Old Testament: the children of Israel, having just triumphantly left Egypt after centuries of slavery and oppression, are literally backed into a corner with the Egyptian army bearing down on them fast. The people begin to doubt, murmur and complain, but what does their leader, Moses, do? How does Moses respond to a nation filled with doubters? Moses says,

> *"Do not fear! Stand by and see the salvation of the LORD which He will accomplish for you today; the Egyptians whom you have seen today, you will never see them again forever. The LORD will fight for you while you keep silent"* (Exod. 14:13-14).

If we ever hope to really bask in the unfathomable faithfulness of God, we must believe. We must have unwavering confidence in God's ability to come through when most needed. Our faith must overcome doubt.

Speak to Your Mountain

In verse 23 of this passage we are commanded to speak to the mountain. How does a person speak about something he is seeing through the eyes of faith before it ever becomes reality?

Real faith is placing so much confidence in God that you speak as if the answer has already come even though physical eyes cannot yet see. You become fully persuaded that your prayers will be answered before they actually are.

Several months ago I had a board meeting in East Texas for No Compromise Ministries. As I prayed over the agenda for that meeting I kept sensing the Lord saying, "You need to go and listen." I obeyed, but it was kind of awkward sitting in a room full of board members and telling them our only agenda was for me to listen to anything they had to say to me. Most of them had nothing to say. One woman felt the Lord impressing her to call me to lead FBC Paradise to be a house of prayer.

By the time the meeting ended it was getting late, and I made arrangements to stay in what I affectionately call my "prayer cabin," near Palestine, which is about seventy-five minutes northwest of Lufkin. The cabin is located on some property managed by a treasured brother in Christ whose boss has allowed me to use it occasionally over the years. I cherished the time I would get to spend in that cabin, but I knew my time would be short. I wanted to get all that I could from the Lord before I had to leave around lunch the following day. I read long into the wee hours of the morning and tried to get up as soon as my eyes popped open, eager and expectant to have a significant encounter with the Lord before returning to my family and FBC Paradise. While having my quiet time that morning, I sensed another message from the Lord: "When I told you to come and listen, I was not just talking about the board meeting."

Over the years, I have had a hard time listening to the Lord, so by no stretch of the imagination am I claiming to be an expert. So when I sensed God's directive I opened my Bible and began to read, but I did not get anything out of that. Next, I moved to a different chair, leaned my head back, and offered a prayer to the Lord: "Lord, I want to listen to You, but I am not good at this. Please help me to hear what You have to say." After that brief prayer I tried to clear my mind and just listen. At first my mind continued to think of the church and spit out random thoughts, but in time I was able to sit before the Lord and be open to what He had to say. My pulse slowed, my thoughts settled, and I actually was able to rest before the Lord with an open heart and a quiet mind. Soon He began to speak some things to me—profound things. Most of what He spoke to me that November morning revolved around prayer, and I wrote every word of it in my journal, which I often reread to this day to remind me how to pray. Some of what He spoke was for me alone, while other things He spoke related to our church. At that time we were searching for a youth minister and were without a permanent music minister as well. Our search committee had been meeting and praying, but they did not sense the Lord's leading in regard to any of the resumes they had been through.

During that time of listening to God, one name surfaced in my mind—Darrell Fishbeck. I knew Darrell from past ministry events but also knew that he was happy where he had been serving for almost six years, in his home church in his hometown of Blanco, Texas. Darrell had no reason in the world to want to move, but while in my chair in the prayer cabin that morning I sensed the Lord saying to me, "Darrell Fishbeck is the man I have appointed to be youth minister of your church. He is comfortable where he is, but if you will lead the committee to fast and pray, I will lead him to you."

When our search committee met later the next week, I shared what I had sensed the Lord saying to me in that cabin, and I was amazed to discover that they had heard the same word from the Lord. We committed to fast and pray for Darrell and his wife, Charissa. Darrell, who had been approached about the job by this time, was quite frank in telling us that he was happy where he was and was not looking to move, but the committee continued to fast and pray and asked him to come to Paradise for an interview. Darrell and Charissa agreed to come, but Darrell told us up front that he had not heard the Lord telling Him to leave

Blanco. As Darrell tells it, upon driving into the community of Paradise for that interview he commented to Charissa, "This doesn't feel like home."

Darrell, Charissa, and I visited before the interview in my office, and I drove them around town (which didn't take long). When Darrell asked me what I would do if he didn't feel a call to Paradise, I told him that I would just put a *yet* on the end of that statement and that I was fully assured that God had appointed them to our church. I did not meet with the search committee that night during the near three-hour interview because I did not want to try to sway either side in the process. I had told them what the Lord had shown me, and I trusted Him to the rest.

Darrell and Charissa drove back home after the interview, and the Lord must have ridden with them, because I received a phone call from Darrell the next day, asking what the next step was. Today they are on the field in Paradise serving passionately and being a grand blessing to our ministry team and have just celebrated their one-year anniversary here at FBC Paradise. It was an amazing journey for them to get here, and we have all been able to behold God's faithfulness over and over again.

Our search committee had prayed and fasted over the course of several months, believing that God had called the Fishbecks to serve in our church. We were absolutely convinced that we had heard from God and that Darrell and Charissa, along with their children, Hayley, Peyton, and Easton, would be a part of our team. In the beginning, Darrell gave no signs of encouragement, but we kept praying and believing until it was a done deal.

Faith is when you act in the present as if something you have seen through eyes of faith in the spiritual realm is already manifested in the physical realm. Often God is honored when you speak of the prayer request as if it were done before you ever lay your physical eyes on the results of the miracle.

I recall doing this very thing in a message one night about the publication of a book I had written, trusting God that I would someday see it on the shelves of a local bookstore. I spoke that vision by faith but can still remember the joy I felt when I walked into two different bookstores in Lufkin, Texas, and saw two books I had written sitting on the shelves. What I had spoken by faith became fact as God answered that prayer. Now my faith has been strengthened in this area and I can trust Him to make a way to publish this book as well.

One of the meanings of the word *say* is "to break silence."[5] There are multitudes of things existing in the spiritual realm that God has spoken by faith into the physical realm. Currently I have a list of three lost men I am pleading with God to save. I have spoken in one prayer group about my belief that God is going to save the souls of all of those men. A few people snickered, but when one of those men recently began attending services periodically, many more began to believe. We have seen breakthroughs in the lives of family members of the second man, and by faith we speak to the mountain of unbelief in these men's hearts and believe they will *all* embrace Jesus Christ as Savior. Let us not be afraid to speak to our mountains and break the silence on what God intends to do.

A word of caution is necessary here: we had better be *sure* we have heard from God clearly before we go speaking to mountains publicly. The proof of our having heard from God is that our prayers are answered and we get to see the very thing we have been trusting God for and speaking about by faith.

---

5 *Bible Soft PC Study Bible version 4.20* (1988-2004).

Believe

The word *believe* has already been highlighted (Mark 11:24), but the word can mean to "think to be true," "be persuaded," "have conviction," "trust," and "place confidence in." When we pray or hear others praying, do you hear this conviction and belief in their petitions? If we are not persuaded or do not have conviction that we are going to receive what we are praying for, our prayers are just an exercise in futility.

I used to meet with a group of men on Monday mornings to pray. When I prayed with those men, I felt their conviction, trust, and confidence that God would answer; in fact, they prayed *expecting* answers. What a special band of brothers! Now I pray with group from our church every Monday evening at 7 p.m., and that prayer meeting is one of the highlights of my week. We pray with conviction and confidence, and the Lord has honored those prayers.

We must *believe* when we pray if we are to receive anything from the Lord. When faith soars to this degree, nothing is impossible—souls are saved, dead churches are brought back to life, disciples are equipped, marriages are healed, and families are restored. Belief must precede and sustain prayer. When Christians enter into this kind of praying, miracles are sure to follow and mountains must move. The Scriptures declare this to be true.

How do we get to this level of belief? Though there are many avenues to this kind of faith, I will suggest three.

Immerse Yourself in the Word

I cannot reiterate this point enough. The more you soak in the Scriptures, the greater confidence you have in God. You cannot peruse the pages of Scripture and not see the power of

God on display in both the Old and New Testaments. Each time you gain a nugget of truth and chew on it for soul nourishment, your faith increases. The more you are immersed in the Word, the stronger that faith grows and the deeper the roots of endurance sink into the soil of complete trust in our sovereign God, no matter what you might be facing.

Therefore, when you need great faith in God, you can go to the vault of Scriptures you have deposited into your heart and mind over and over again. When doubt begins to surface, it can quickly be uprooted by the reminder of some truth treasured in your heart (Ps. 119:11).

Read Christian Biographies

Other than the reading of Scripture, nothing has done more to bolster my faith in God than reading about the lives of the prayer giants of the past. I have already mentioned many of them in the introduction of this chapter.

Try reading about the lives of E. M. Bounds, Reese Howells, Robert McMurray McCheyne, Leonard Ravenhill, John Hyde, Hudson Taylor, and A. W. Tozer. That would be a pretty good start, but there are others, like Amy Carmichael, Joni Eareckson Tada, Martin Luther, and George Mueller, whose life stories also make for fascinating reading. These are men and women who saw miracles and who prayed for the advancement of God's kingdom.

I never fail to be inspired to be a greater man of prayer and to believe God for greater things after reading about the lives of these great saints. As you do the same, I believe God will fan the smoldering embers of your prayer life and give you greater trust in Him. Don't idolize these men and women, but learn from them and put what you learn into practice.

Fellowship with People of Large Faith

Over the years, I have sought to surround myself with people of large faith. These are the people I want in my inner circle. These are men and women who believe that nothing is too difficult for the Lord. These are the people I worship with and the people who make up the board of directors for No Compromise Ministries. When I am around people like this, my faith is ignited and encouraged because they pray large prayers and expect large answers. Just last night, I was talking on the sidewalk out in front of our church with a woman who serves on our board. As we discussed our NCM newsletter, I told her I had a vision of seeing that newsletter eventually sent out to over 10,000 people. She did not blink but affirmed her belief in the Lord to make that happen. Her affirmation meant that much more to me because of what I know about that woman and her prayer life.

On the other hand, when I spend too much time around people of small faith and "stinking thinking," even the smallest hills begin to look like mountains to me. I become discouraged and easily sink into despair. Before long I have a defeated attitude and my prayer life is stifled. I can tell you firsthand that it makes a huge difference when you keep a strong inner circle of faith titans close to you to stimulate and encourage your faith and to help you tower over every mountain that stands in your path.

Conclusion

When we were first contacted by the pastor search committee of First Baptist Church of Paradise, Texas (located near Decatur and northwest of Fort Worth), Brenda and I began looking at the housing market in that area. To our disappointment we found that houses were quite a bit more expensive in Paradise than in East Texas. But the Lord moved the process along, and soon we found ourselves making the move to Paradise to take up the pastorate at the church. Not long after moving into the parsonage, Brenda's van broke down repeatedly, and the equity from our house in East Texas (which sold quickly) was used to purchase not only the truck I mentioned earlier but also a new vehicle for Brenda. Just like *that* we had no money for a down payment on a house. We contented ourselves with living in the church parsonage until we could save money for a house, and we therefore put house hunting on the back burner.

One day while driving from a fast food restaurant, I sensed the Lord asking me a question: "Why did you quit believing Me for a house?" I really did not have an answer. I had believed the Lord for our house in Hudson, Texas, but quit asking when we moved to Paradise. Purchasing a house didn't seem feasible at the time, so I put it out of my mind.

A few months later, after a sweet season of prayer, the Lord spoke to me again. "Matt, I desire to give you a house in Paradise. Trust Me for it." That was His entire message— no specifics, just exhortation to keep trusting God for a house. Only a few days ago, this prayer burden began to intensify in my heart.

Ever since then I have been praying and asking God for a house. I guess you could say we are actively "house hunting"; we have driven all over the community multiple times looking at houses, we have set a few appointments with realtors, and we have searched the papers and Internet.

We have prayed and waited over three years at this point. We continue to ask the Lord for His direction and for His provision. Until that time we are content to wait on Him. Please do not doubt for one moment that in our waiting we have quit believing. We continually pray over our situation. "Delight yourself in the Lord and He will give you the desires of your heart," (Ps 37:4).

I know God has a house for my family. I do not know the location of the house. I do not know the color of the bricks or siding. I only know that God has spoken His promise to provide my family with housing of our own in His time and not mine.

Whatever mountains stand in the way of that prayer becoming reality will move. I know God will intervene and bring glory to His name in this situation. I have seen Him do it before and we rejoice even now that we will see Him do it again.

This morning as I was having a devotional with my boys before going to school I talked to them about faith and what it meant. They said it simply meant trusting God or believing God. I read from Hebrews 11:32-34:

> And what more shall I say? For time will fail me if I tell of Gideon, Barak, Samson, Jephthah, of David and Samuel and the prophets, who by faith conquered kingdoms, performed acts of righteousness, obtained promises, shut the mouths of lions, quenched the power of fire, escaped the edge of the sword, from weakness were made strong, became mighty in war, put foreign armies to flight.

I'd like to conclude this story with a mountain moving prayer that was answered in this church. Not long after coming here we really began to see the limitations of our facilities. First Baptist Church is land locked. We do have enough room for our small groups, parking or worship. We have no space to build on and yet our church continues to grow. Many of the classrooms are pushed to capacity and beyond with swelling attendance.

A team was formed in our church to look into this issue and to discern God's will about what we should do. For over two years this group met praying diligently for God to reveal His direction and plans. We discussed and prayed over every option. We talked about buying property adjacent to the church to add more space. We discussed going to two worship services on Sunday mornings which we eventually did do. We conversed about doing the same thing for our overcrowded Sunday School classes and going to two Sunday School hours. No one ever felt a peace about that option. There was even discussion about bringing in some portable buildings for classes to meet in, but with our parking situation already over-crowded that did not seem like a logical solution.

One option always seemed to surface and that was to relo-cate the church. I felt in my heart that was what we should do but dreaded the thought of trying to lead the church through that process. Relocating churches has caused a great deal of division in more than one congregation. On top of that was the mountain-like obstacle of raising money, not only for the land to relocate to, but also for building new facilities. We prayed more and waited for God to reveal His plan.

For two years we prayed and waited on God to show us what to do. During this time the crowding problem con-tinued. We often heard comments from people when they would come to visit that they could not find a place to park. At one point we were using every available classroom in the church and one class met in a house near the church in the home of one of our deacons.

After asking God for wisdom during that two year stretch, the Long Range Planning Team finally discerned that the Lord was leading our church to buy two houses next to the church to serve as an interim step before buying land and relocating. We presented the proposal to the church on a Sunday morning in the spring of 2008 and could not have foreseen how the Lord was going to move a seemingly impossible mountain right before our very eyes.

The Long Range Planning Team asked me to preach a message on faith and trusting God on the Sunday they presented their proposal of buying the two houses next to the church. I preached a message from Mark 6 about the loaves and fish and God's provision. Unknown to any of us, God was using this message in the heart of one man in a profound way.

The following Monday I received a phone call from this man the Lord spoke to in a powerful fashion asking me to set up a meeting. When we met the next day he drove me and a member from The Long Range Planning Team to a prime piece of property he owned and told us the Lord had led him to donate ten acres to the church. He informed us he did not want to make a big fuss over it and did not want any recognition. He was simply being obedient to the Lord. He just wanted the assurance that the church would use the property to build on and not turn around and sell it.

I was dumbfounded. In my wildest dreams I could not have imagined such a scenario. What had seemed nearly impossible only weeks and months earlier now was a mountain moved right before our very eyes. Nothing is impossible with God!

We informed the church and called for a month of prayer about what the Lord was asking us to do. To vote to accept the gift of the ten acres was also a vote to relocate the church.

We held a meeting to answer questions from the congregation and then set the vote. The congregation seemed to be in support of God leading our church to a new location with expanded facilities. Prayer saturated that business meeting. When it was all said and done, the overwhelming majority voted to relocate the church with very few voting in opposition. I wish it had been a unanimous vote but it was clear that the majority of the congregation sensed the Lord leading us to accept the generous offer of the ten acres and to relocate the First Baptist Church of Paradise.

Today we are walking through the process of determining what type of facilities the Lord is calling us to build and how much money it will cost along with how we will trust the Lord for the money to build those facilities.

God still moves mountains. He still answers prayers in stunningly powerful ways. God still leaves His children staggered at His creative genius in leading His church and children past mountain-like problems and obstacles. No amount of meetings with brilliant business minds could have figured out what to do with our space limitations and know God's heart without prayer. God did more in one thirty minute message than our planning team was able to figure out in over two years. He moved a mountain that seemed immovable.

I urge you, child of God, to keep believing the Lord and His promises in your situation. Your mountain is just as moveable by His powerful hands as ours was. You may have to wait but in the long run, the waiting will all seem worthwhile when you watch God turn your mountain into a mole hill. Beholding God's faithfulness from this vantage point is a beautiful sight.

CHAPTER 6

Prayer that Exceeds Expectations

Now to Him who is able to do exceedingly abundantly above all that we ask or think, according to the power that works in us, to Him be glory in the church by Christ Jesus to all generations, forever and ever. Amen (Eph. 3:20-21 NKJV).

I am a big dreamer, I always have been, but for the longest time I struggled with these verses. You see, I can believe, ask, and imagine the Lord doing a *lot*. My prayers have been large at times, and my confidence has not been in my ability to pray but in God's ability to answer. I'm not afraid to ask the Lord for large things, because large things give God large amounts of glory. Several times, though, I have been disappointed. Many of my large prayers did not translate into the miraculous power of God being as visible as I had hoped. I have been disappointed in my prayer life more times than I can count, but all of that changed on October 16, 2005. I will tell you that story at the end of this chapter; it was a miracle day like none I had seen before.

The question is, why don't we believe God to do *more*, to exceed our small and petty prayers? I know how often my faith and prayers have been tiny when God longs to display His power and glory among the people of this earth. We are all guilty of praying tiny prayers, while God yearns to set people on their ears as they witness His superabundant ability to intervene in the ordinary affairs of life.

I have been greatly convicted of this truth over the past week. When the Lord called us over three years ago to Paradise to serve the First Baptist Church, I had no great vision. In fact, for the first time in my ministry, I could not get a specific vision from the Lord. I prayed, I sought, I listened, and I asked God to paint a portrait of His dream for that church on my heart, but I heard nothing in response. I could see little things along the way, but even after six months of serving the church I had no real vision.

I began setting some personal goals for myself and for the church. Some goals were for increased numerical attendance, while other goals were for seeing people saved and baptized. In hindsight I can see that my goals were rather small because I was being cautious. I had set gargantuan goals in the past only to watch us fall miserably short in petitions. So now that I was pastoring First Baptist Paradise, I decided not to get my hopes up too quickly. I figured that any growth would be a slow and gradual process, and I even began to resign myself to the fact that perhaps God's plans for me included serving in a small church for my entire ministry, something I had to learn to accept.

At the time we had about 50 to 60 people showing up for Sunday school and just a few more for church. I had aspirations of breaking the 100 mark, and my largest dreams included growing to 200 in Sunday school. That goal looked extremely large. But I had read Scriptures that flowed through my heart like burning flames, setting my soul on fire. Even so, at times my faith remained weak. You may ask, how can this be? When you read a verse like Ephesians 3:20, how can you have feeble faith and pray putrid prayers? God is able—He is more than able. He yearns to put His power and His glory on full display for the world to see.

The possibilities of what God can do are *endless*. Think about that for a moment. As a human being, I know my limitations. I get physically tired, emotionally drained, mentally fatigued. But God does not.

> *Do you not know? Have you not heard? The Everlasting God, the LORD, the Creator of the ends of the earth Does not become weary or tired. His understanding is inscrutable. He gives strength to the weary, And to him who lacks might He increases power* (Isa. 40:28-29).

Ponder that verse for a moment—this great God is *everlasting*. He never had a beginning and will never have an ending. He always has been and always will be God, *the* God, who with a word spoke creation into existence. By His simple breath He breathed life into Adam and has woven little boys and girls in the wombs of their mothers ever since. This God who set mountains in place, who carved out the depths of the seas without even the hint of sweat on His brow, is still able to do all that and more. This is the God who never sleeps or wearies, who has wisdom and understanding that supersedes every computer in the world, even surpassing the great "networks."

> "*For My thoughts are not your thoughts, Nor are your ways My ways,' declares the LORD. 'For as the heavens are higher than the earth, So are My ways higher than your ways And My thoughts than your thoughts*'" (Isa. 55:8-9).

God sits on the throne of this universe in sovereignty and chooses to make Himself, His power, His wisdom, and His understanding available to us. Now, think about the kind of prayers you have offered up of late—do they seem small and insignificant in comparison? I know mine do. I am mainly referring to prayers for the expansion of God's kingdom.

Getting back to my prayers for FBC Paradise, I was recently loaned some preaching tapes, which I listened to on my way to a lunch meeting in a town about forty miles from Paradise. While I was driving up Highway 287 North, God met with me in the cab of my truck and shook me out of my sleepy little ministry and my safe ministry dreams. I was convicted, humbled, awed, and stunned by His working in my heart. I was broken, because God held up a mirror before me to show how weak my faith was and how small my prayers had been. I sat in the parking lot listening to that tape, staggered by the mighty blow of God to my heart. It is has now been five days since I first listened to those tapes, and I am still in a state of shock. No message I have ever heard has impacted me as deeply as that message did.

When God began to reveal His vision for First Baptist Paradise in response to that recorded message, I was blown away. I have seen just a glimpse of His power—His abundant, supernatural, incomprehensible, and miraculous power. He allowed me just a glimpse into His vision for my life, family, and ministry, and my mind is still reeling from His revelation. He wants to do so much more than I had been asking for, and His dreams make mine look insignificant, petty, small, miniscule, minute, and miniature.

If we could just get hold of Ephesians 3:20, the implications for the Church, for missions' advancement, for the transformation of whole nations, and for massive spiritual awakenings to spread like a wildfire over parched pastures would be inconceivable. God has done this time and time again in the history of this world, when He decided to grab hold of and shake the hearts of His men and women. First of all, these people would really begin to pray and seek God. They would earnestly believe God for the impossible, and they offered large prayers with huge results that could only come from God. Often God rewarded such praying with power that changed the moral climate of a city, region, or at times a whole nation. On more than one occasion that strong move of God would affect more than one nation and literally impact the world. Where did it start? With someone who really believed that Ephesians 3:20 could be fleshed out in contemporary culture.

God's power has not diminished. He is not in the twilight years of His existence. God is still "in His prime," as He ever will be. God is a strong warrior and a valiant champion on behalf of His children—in tip-top shape, ready, more than able, and superabundantly strengthened to surpass our wildest and largest prayers.

God is ready to stun. God stands ever-prepared to respond to our faith-filled praying. He longs to blow us away with His power. He yearns to glorify Himself in your life and mine.

I listened to those tapes over and over again these past several days. I found myself prostrate before the Lord Wednesday night after Bible study, pleading with God to allow me to serve as pastor in our church for a long time. As God opened His desires for our church and unfolded His dream, I realized that it would take a lifetime to see that dream fulfilled. I asked God for contentment and for tenacious endurance in this church, and I asked Him to take any other call off my life to serve as a pastor and to release in me forever the desire for greener pastures in ministry.

What I have discovered is that God's dream and desires have far exceeded my wildest imagination for FBC Paradise. My initial attendance goals have been shattered in my mind and heart as well as in reality. In fact, God's dream is literally ten times bigger than my dream, and it's bigger than any dream I have ever had for ministry. Yet when God does it— and He will—He will get the glory. He will show a sleepy Christian age that His power is beyond comprehension. He will show pastors that if they would quit running on the performance and program treadmill, appearing busy but not gaining any ground, He could intervene in their churches and communities as they pray and lead their people to pray as well.

The time is past for small faith and miniscule praying. We must get hold of the fact that God longs to do more for His Church than any of us can conceive. What limits Him? The answer is that He can do no mighty work among us because of *our unbelief!* We doubt, make excuses, and refuse to step out of the safety of our boats by faith onto the crashing waves of our circumstances.

I urge you to sit before the Lord and allow Him to take the juices of this verse and let them ooze down your spiritual throat until you savor every drop. May we arise from those divine encounters no longer as people dreaming our own dreams but rather as men and women yielded, empowered, and equipped with hefty fearless faith that unleashes the power of God in our lives, ministries, families, and churches.

I told you I would share a personal story with you to illustrate a time in my ministry when God made Ephesians 3:20 come to life right before my very eyes. I need to give you some background to set the context. I had heard about the First Baptist Church of Paradise when my college roommate mentioned my name to a co-worker of someone who worked with a member of the FBC Paradise pastor search committee. I received an e-mail from the chairperson of that committee asking if I would send a resume, but I really was not interested at the time. After being turned down by thirty-two other churches in the span of a year and a half, I was weary of the whole process and very disillusioned with the way Baptist churches select pastors.

I sent a resume anyway and began doing some investigative work about the church, but what I dug up was not pleasant. The church had a bad reputation and had recently gone through a church-wide split over some staff issues. In the aftermath, church attendance had plummeted and the morale of the church had ebbed to an all-time low. To top it all off, the church finances were in disarray.

When I discovered all this, I could not have been less interested in going to that church. At the time, Brenda and I knew that we had been released by the Lord to leave East Texas, but no doors had opened for us yet. In fact, as I mentioned earlier, well over thirty doors had shut formally in our faces. So we continued our ministry with the CentrePointe Community Church (a church we started in our house) with a little over a dozen people coming each week.

Other opportunities came our way, and as we watched each door close we realized that FBC Paradise was still out there, waiting. The search committee asked if I would send a preaching tape, which I did, and as the e-mails kept coming I kept asking questions to learn what I could about the church and the community. Deep down I still was not interested, partly because I had my sights set on another church where I already knew the music minister and two people on the search committee. It seemed like a slam dunk—except for the fact that Brenda did not have peace about our serving there. Strangely enough, she felt more drawn to the Paradise church.

On a preaching trip to West Texas I decided to drive through the Paradise community, which was far out of the way, but I needed to visualize this thing we were praying about. As I expected, the community was small with very little in it. I was impressed with the school facilities, and the church building looked well kept, but I knew the trouble the church had been through, and I really did not want to jump into that headache. The truth is, I was having a hard time visualizing myself as the pastor of *any* "First Baptist Church." Most of the First Baptist churches I had known were legalistic, divided, disgruntled, and volatile, none of which looked appealing to me.

Soon the Paradise church called to set up an interview. I began getting calls from people who were on my list of references, telling me they had been contacted by the Paradise search committee. One Sunday morning Brenda and I made arrangements for the children, I preached at the CentrePointe service, and then we hit the trail running to make the five-hour trip to Paradise to meet with the search committee in the early afternoon.

Upon arriving at the church we were met by the search committee, made up of five men and women and two alternates. During the interview process I asked some difficult questions and fielded many questions as well, all of which I answered unflinchingly and in a straightforward manner. The interview had to be cut short, however, because the committee had scheduled me to preach in a church about an hour away in order to hear me preach live.

In an awkward move, the members of the committee asked Brenda and me to ride with them in the church van to the other location. We found this very odd since we had assumed that we would be driving our own vehicle. Although we were disconcerted at first, that ride gave us a chance to get to know the committee members better, which was valuable. I preached a hard word in front of that committee that night, trying not to impress them but to facilitate a mighty move of God in the service.

On the drive back to Paradise, I noticed a lot of conversation in the back but not much where Brenda was sitting. I had just about decided that the committee had hated the message and that this was going to be another closed door, so I was completely unprepared when we returned to the sanctuary of FBC Paradise that evening and the search committee chairman boldly extended an invitation for us to come in view of a call. Once again Brenda and I were caught off guard but for a different reason; though our seating arrangement on the ride back to the church had left us no time to communicate, it was obvious in that moment to both Brenda and me that God had indeed called us to serve at FBC Paradise. We accepted the invitation right there on the spot. Several weeks later we came in view of a call, and we celebrated with the church when the vote to hire us was affirmative.

My first Sunday as the pastor of the First Baptist Church of Paradise was Father's Day—June 16, 2005. I received that blessing as my Father God's gift to me after the longest and hardest season of my ministry. I knew, however, that our work was cut out for us, because attendance the Sunday prior to our arrival had plummeted to thirty-eight!

For a year, my primary focus was to fulfill the Lord's directive to love those people and to preach the Word. My expectations were not too high; in fact, my attendance goals at the time were very low. Over the first few months, attendance increased little by little to a point nine months later when we boasted fifty to sixty in Sunday school. Thanks to my four-year experience shepherding a tiny flock of a dozen people back in East Texas, I was content with the modest growth and the slightly increased attendance. I had never been the pastor of a church larger than seventy-five in number anyway, so my expectations were not great.

Following that good old Baptist tradition, we set aside October 16, 2005, as a high-attendance Sunday. We did our best to promote it and set a lofty goal of 120 for that day, which was really a stretch for this band of believers. We prayed and I cast vision, meaning that I tried to paint a mental picture of reaching our goal while seeking to rally everyone around that goal. I knew that the only way we would even come near that attendance goal would be by a direct intervention by the Lord. According to attendance records, it had been decades since the church had seen that many in attendance for Sunday school. To attract the community, we planned a punt, pass, and kick competition for the children along with bounce houses, an inflatable obstacle course, and other activities to fill the afternoon after the morning service. I did my best to rally the troops and pump them up as the date got closer and closer.

Let me remind you, our church had not broken 100 in attendance in the several months we had been there. I was nervous about the goal, but I challenged our church members. Every time I went out in the community I invited people, putting many of them on the spot and challenging them to come help us reach our goal. I was determined to not be denied.

October 16th arrived, and the trickle of people coming in the doors of the church quickly became a steady stream—many of the people I had invited, along with scores of people that we had never seen before. There was genuine excitement in the air as the classrooms began to fill and it was apparent that whether we met our goal or not, our people had tried their hardest. We had to scramble to find extra chairs for the packed Sunday school rooms.

I waited nervously in my office for the final tally, and when the Sunday school directors passed by my door on their way to putting up the numbers on our attendance sign, I asked how we had done. I'll always remember the sight of that precious gem of a lady smiling at me and saying those unbelievable words: *"Two hundred and seven!"* Sure enough, God had drawn 207 people to our Sunday school on that morning. He had obliterated our puny attendance goal! I found out later that it was the highest attendance for Sunday school in the history of the church!

On top of that, God once again flexed His divine muscles and showed His power through the faithful givers of our church. We took in a $10,000 offering that day, more than tripling our normal offerings. In that moment, God showed me the true power of Ephesians 3:20. In my wildest dreams I thought the church might possibly grow to 200 one day after many years of hard labor and praying, but God showed me on that day that my dream did not match His dream. He is able to do *exceedingly* more than we can ask or even imagine. Nothing is impossible with our God.

Since that Sunday, we have only gone under 100 a few times and have recently moved to two Sunday morning worship services, yet God has shown me that His dreams for our church supersede even that high-attendance day. It is hard for me to put this down on paper because I know many will doubt what I have heard from God, but I have sensed the Lord showing me 1,000 people being the minimum of His plan for FBC Paradise. Logistically, we can barely hold 200 in Sunday school and our sanctuary can fit around 250 people comfortably. So how can God take a church from 38 to 1,000 in attendance? That is impossible, and as for me, I have never even aspired to shepherd a church that large. But the whole point is that this is of God, and when God does it, *everyone will know He did it*! *God* will get the glory!

When I sit back and take all this in, I am humbled and dazed—especially when I think that I did not even want to come to FBC Paradise. God knew what He was doing, and I see now that God has been preparing me for this church my whole life as a Christian. God has performed a ministry marriage between these precious people and me as their pastor. I also think about the fact that if 1,000 people is the minimum of what God desires to do in the Paradise community and in this church, if God is superabundantly able to do more than I think or can even ask, that's just plain *scary*—not in a bad way but in a good way. I have become increasingly aware that I am living a miracle that is only now beginning to unfold.

What about you? Will you allow God to reveal His heart to you? Will you accept His challenge to pray, ask and believe for things only He can do? Will you choose to trust that God is able to supplant all your dreams and prayers with bigger dreams and more God-exalting prayers? If you and I do, we will behold His faithfulness in ways we could have never dreamed or imagined, and God will get much glory!

CHAPTER 7

Praying with Tears

In those days Hezekiah became mortally ill. And Isaiah the prophet the son of Amoz came to him and said to him, "Thus says the Lord, set your house in order for you shall die and not live." Then he turned his face to the wall and prayed to the Lord saying, "Remember now, O Lord, I beseech You, how I have walked before You in truth and with a whole heart and have done what is good in Your sight." And Hezekiah wept bitterly. Before Isaiah had gone out of the middle court, the word of the Lord came to him saying, "Return and say to Hezekiah the leader of my people, 'Thus says the Lord, the God of your father David, I have heard your prayer, I have seen your tears; behold, I will heal you. On the third day you shall go up to the house of the Lord. I will add fifteen years to your life, and I will deliver you and this city from the hand of the king of Assyria; and I will defend this city for My own sake and for My servant David's sake'" (2 Kings 20:1-6).

Those who sow in tears shall reap with joyful shouting. He who goes to and fro weeping, carrying his bag of seed, Shall indeed come again with a shout of joy, bringing his sheaves with him (Ps. 126:5-6).

An old preacher who lived many years ago was seeing many people saved under his ministry. Not far down the road from this old preacher was a young preacher who admired his elder's evangelistic success. No matter how the young preacher prayed or worked, he did not see the same fruit in his ministry as he saw consistently in the seasoned older pastor's ministry.

One day the young man determined to visit the old preacher to ask what the secret of his success might be. He walked the several-mile journey to visit the older preacher and asked him what he did that made his ministry so successful. The young preacher said, "I pray, I study, I witness, yet *still* I do not see the same results you do. What am I *not* doing in order to see the lost in my community saved?"

The wise old preacher answered with a simple question: "Have you tried tears?"

We do not see many tears in prayer meetings anymore. There is a type of prayer and intercession that can only be achieved with tears and not with words. God yearns to break through our cold and calloused hearts to bring us to places of weeping over the things that break His heart.

Several years ago while I was in full-time evangelism I was listening to some others give testimony about a youth weekend in which I had just participated. (My office at the time was the old abandoned prayer room secluded from all the other offices at the church where I served.) In the course of that meeting we watched a video, which the Lord used to really break my heart. I left the meeting and went to my office, where I pleaded with the Lord to break my heart with the same things that break His heart.

As I prayed, the tears began to flow, and gentle sobbing turned into full-blown weeping. I felt the suffocating burden for the lost, for rampant and unchecked sin, for the impotency of the local church, and for the need for revival. Before long, I sank from my knees to lie prostrate before the Lord—wordless and broken. The tears flowed torrentially and my breathing began to be labored under the oppressive burden I felt from the Lord. This moment is forever etched on the pages of my mind, and even reliving it in order to write it down is a powerful experience. Finally I asked God to stay His hand because I could not stand the oppressive weight of that burden. I have seldom felt burdened the same way since.

On another occasion many years later, a dear brother in the Lord named Joel Perritte and I were in this very prayer cabin where I have retreated to hammer out this book. We were prostrate on the floor in the living room, praying, when both of us were seized with the words of Isaiah 6:8: *"Then I heard the voice of the Lord, saying, 'Whom shall I send, and who will go for Us?' Then I said, 'Here am I. Send me!'"* My heart began to break for the nations of this world who plead with the Lord to send help. I began to weep harder as I thought about pastors in small struggling churches who were on their faces weeping, begging God for strength and aid. I asked the Lord to connect those prayers with our prayers, and a few months later the Lord opened a door for both Joel and me to preach in Cuba. It was a fascinating journey and one that ignited a call for me to continue to travel to the nations to proclaim the love of Jesus and to minister to pastors around the world.

God, Break Our Hearts

Do we have the courage to ask to God to break through the walls of comfort we have built around our hearts, to cause them to ache and yearn and break for the things that grieve His heart? Or will we sleep peacefully night after night while the enemies of darkness work tirelessly and continually to advance the kingdom of darkness? Will our prayers remain tearless? How I pray that God would take our hearts of stone and crush them to powder. We need the Lord to crush our hearts and allow the stream of tears to flow in ceaseless intercessions.

I am not writing about something I am unwilling to endure myself. I live in regret for asking God to stay His hand and remove that burden back in my office at the Denman Avenue Baptist Church in Lufkin, Texas. I have never had another experience of that magnitude, but recently while preaching to a small group of teenagers and adults, my heart became burdened for that event and for Palestine, Texas. I decided then that I want God to weigh me down with His burden for *this* town. I want God to give me His heart for the Paradise community, and I need God to do that.

What I need is to become a broken man in His presence. As a pastor, I need to pray with tears for several men I continue to trust God to save. I need to weep for my country, which has drifted so far away from the truth and from God Himself. Professing to be wise, we as a nation have shown ourselves to be fools (Rom. 1:22).

We must also ask God to break our hearts for the lost. Think of the millions who perish—they *perish!* Each day the lost among us take a step closer to eternal damnation and will receive the full-force fury of God at the moment they leave this life. Daily, people fall headlong into the fiery pit of hell, and yet you and I go about life as normal. Who stands in the gap for them? *"I searched for a man among them who would build up the wall and stand in the gap before Me for the land, so that I would not destroy it; but I found no one"* (Ezek. 22:30). My heart aches when I think of my prayerlessness on behalf of this sin-sickened nation—a nation where abortions are seen as a woman's prerogative, a nation embracing gay marriage and calling it an alternative lifestyle. My soul is grieved over pastors who tickle the ears of their congregations and have proven the prophecy of Amos 8:11-12:

> *"Behold days are coming," declares the Lord GOD, "When I will send a famine on the land, Not a famine for bread or a thirst for water, But rather for hearing the words of the LORD. People will stagger from sea to sea And from the north even to the east; They will go to and fro to seek the word of the LORD, but they will not find it."*

My heart breaks that we are living in such a day. In our efforts to be culturally relevant, positive, and encouraging, vast portions of the Bible are neglected and ignored. Disciples are increasingly becoming shallow in their faith and cannot endure the winds of suffering when they blow in. Sin is not called sin but rather a "poor choice." O God, we need You to break the hearts of pastors in their pulpits, in their studies, and in the seminary classrooms. If God's chosen men do not weep, is it any wonder that there is so little weeping in the pews?

I believe that pastors need to weep over the loss of power in the pulpit. There were times when God used His men like wrecking balls as they preached with voices of thunder. Today there is a famine in the land, and God's people like it so because they enjoy having their ears tickled.

O God, how I plead with You to well up the tears that have long been dammed up in the hearts of your servants. I pray that we would no longer be satisfied with our small successes but would be broken over our failure to impact our communities and watch You transform lives. May we weep over our empty and barren altars and our silent and extinct prayer meetings. May we weep over the plague of divorce ravaging marriages both inside and outside the Church. May tears come from the depths of our souls as we cry, "No more! No longer will we sit smug in our prayer circles satisfied with our faithless ramblings!" May tears accompany our intercession, and may the fires of faith and the tears of brokenness move You, Lord, to release greater power in all that we do. May our cheeks be ever stained with the salt from our tears as we live to make intercession, giving You no rest.

> *On your walls, O Jerusalem, I have appointed watchmen; All day and all night they will never keep silent. You who remind the LORD, take no rest for yourselves; And give Him no rest until He establishes And makes Jerusalem a praise in the earth* (Isa. 62:6-7).

May our worship services move people to tears as You convict of sin and the need of salvation. May teardrops continually stain the carpets of our altars. God, I plead for you to teach us to pray with tears. May our tears move You to perform miracles. May our tears move You to heal the sick, to revive the church, to restore marriages, to start spiritual awakenings, and to call the church to repentance and holiness. May our tears move You to set the captives free, to deepen our affection for You, and to create in us an insatiable hunger for You and Your Word.

God, move us to tears over our casual attitude toward sin in Your house. As Your Word says in 1 Peter 4:17, *"For it is time for judgment to begin with the household of God; if it begins with us first, what will be the outcome for those who do not obey the gospel of God?"* I ask You to bring Your Church to tears over the sins of pornography, alcoholism, lying, gossip, stealing, idolatry, adultery, immorality, and power-mongering.

I ask You to move us to tears that we are biblically illiterate, though we boast in our classes, studies, and preaching. I ask You, O Lord, to move us to weep over the fact that our eyes have remained dry for far too long in prayer. I ask You to give us a deeper compassion for people and help us to be moved as You were moved when You saw the flocks of people distressed and dispirited like sheep without a shepherd (Matt. 9:36).

In Psalm 126:5-6 at the beginning of our chapter, pay special attention to the word *tears* and the word *weeping*. *Tears* means "to cry" while *weeping* means "to bewail." As we go about and sow gospel seeds in the hearts of people, we must fertilize our witness with tears and prayer. If we do, we shall come back rejoicing when those we prayed for and travailed in prayer over are saved and transformed. There will be great celebration after we have sown gospel seed in the hearts of lost men and lost women by faith with the flow of tears mingled in.

In March of 2008 I had the privilege of traveling to Saskatchewan up in Canada to work with our mission church in the little town of Humboldt, located about an hour west of Saskatoon. It was a fast trip as we arrived on a Friday and came back home on a Monday. We traveled a great deal and had a series of meetings to plan and network with other pastors for future trips. We met with the First Baptist Church of Humboldt, a small but tenacious group of believers who believe God called them to plant a church three years ago even though they have never had a pastor on Sunday morning.

After worshipping with those wonderful people on Sunday morning and getting to lead the services, we ate a quick lunch and then drove back to Saskatoon where we spent the night in order to catch our early morning flight back to Dallas, TX the next day.

I went downstairs to the large lobby area of the Saskatoon Inn soon after getting settled into our room to do some praying and reflecting on all we had learned and experienced during our trip. Darrell, our student and worship minister, and Corbin, our ministry intern, and myself eventually all ended up back in our room on the eighth floor. As I stood at the window looking out over the lights of downtown Saskatoon my heart began to break. All I could think about was how many people do not know the Savior and how pastors must feel overwhelmed by the enormity of the challenge before them. I asked the guys to join me in a prayer time before we went out for dinner.

In the beginning the prayer time seemed forced and ritualistic. Soon the presence of God invaded our eighth floor room and settled onto our broken hearts. We wept for the lostness of Humboldt, Saskatoon, the province of Saskatchewan, the whole nation of Canada and back home for Paradise, TX. We felt sorrow for the millions upon millions across that great nation and our own who do not have any relationship with Jesus Christ. It really pained my heart as we interceded for those two nations. The heaviness and weightiness of that prayer meeting is beyond my ability to capture with words. Suffice to say we were in God's glorious presence and our hearts were melting.

Soon the tears fell like a torrential rain storm. Puddles began to form, our breathing became labored, our eyes began to burn from the salt in the tears, our cheeks were moistened with the steady hot flow of our hearts being poured out like liquid to God in intercession for that nation. That prayer meeting was the highlight of that trip for me personally and stands out as a sacred encounter with the Lord as well as one of the highlights of my entire ministry. I believe the Lord heard our prayers and that He also saw our tears and will move powerfully.

Do tears mixed with confident praying move God to action? It did in Hezekiah's situation. Notice what the Lord says in response to Hezekiah's tear-saturated prayer: *"I have heard your prayer, I have seen your tears; behold, I will heal you. On the third day you shall go up to the house of the LORD"* (2 Kings 20:5).

Yes, God hears prayer. He heard Hezekiah's prayer just like He hears yours and mine. Yet God did not stop there; He mentioned the fact that He saw the tears that fell from the cheeks of that leader. He was moved equally by Hezekiah's tears and Hezekiah's prayer. Prayer and tears are powerful weapons in the hands of God.

A friend recently told me about an experience he had on a mission trip deep into Mexico. His group traveled into the mountainous region of Mexico to minister to a group that most people do not even know exist. While there among those people, my friend was introduced to an older man who was known for his prayer life, and the members of my friend's mission group were invited to join this seasoned saint for a time of prayer. As he looked at where the elderly man knelt beside a chair, my friend noticed discolored spots all over the chair and the floor. As the older man began to pray for the people of his community, he began to weep as if his heart was broken. After the prayer time ended, my friend said it suddenly dawned on him that the stains on the chair and floor were from many years' worth of tears—tears of grief, broken-ness, and a desperate desire for the Lord to move.

What about your floor, or mine? There are no tear stains in my office or in my chair at home where I pray. Dear God, I plead with You, help us learn how to pray with tears. We are not asking for some trumped-up experience that makes us look good or more spiritual than other people. We are looking for Your heart and Your burden to be put upon us. We are looking for You to move in our midst and to draw the anguish of soul for those without Christ and the broken and shattered lives all around. We want to weep in prayer over those who suffer from physical illness or the emotional pain of a broken heart, who have been forced to say good-bye to loved ones before they were ready. We pray for tears to weep for children who are neglected, unloved, unwanted, and uncared for. We pray for tears for the nations of this world without churches, without Bibles, without preachers, teachers, and missionaries. May we often find ourselves in tears as we pray. May Your compassion for people consume our souls and draw us into deeper levels of intercession than we have ever known before.

Lord, this is not something we can manufacture on our own. If You do not break through our hearts, we will con-tinue to pray tearless prayers that do not produce miracles or cause the world to sit up and take notice of You. You have our hearts, and we now ask You to break through them and to cover them with Your heart for this world. May we never pray the same again. Amen.

CHAPTER 8

Bold Prayer

Therefore let us draw near with confidence to the throne of grace, so that we may receive mercy and find grace to help in time of need (Heb. 4:16).

When Brenda and I go to a mall or a store, it never ceases to amaze me how persistent our boys can be in asking for this or that. We were recently in the Grapevine Mills Mall, in Grapevine, Texas, when our second son, Tanner, noticed a glow-in-the-dark fluorescent miniature golf course. He was fascinated, and for the next hour he kept asking me if we could play. He had no reservations in his asking but pleaded with me over and over again to let him and his brothers play a round of golf. There was no fear and no timidity in his asking. He was bold and persistent.

How is it that a nine-year-old boy can be bold in making his request to his earthly father but we are so timid in making our requests made known to our Heavenly Father? God *loves* us; we are His children. God loves to bless His children, just as we who are parents love to bless our children. God does not always give us what we ask, but He gives what is for our good. So why do we not take this Scripture to heart?

God invites us to draw near, to approach Him with boldness and confidence. It is not that we come on any merit of our own. Who are you and I to come into the presence of God and make demands of Him? On our own merit we are "nobodies" and therefore have no rights or privileges. But when we accept Jesus as our Savior, our status changes completely. We become heirs, children of the King, forgiven, redeemed, and made righteous in Him. "*He made Him who knew no sin to be sin on our behalf, so that we might become the righteousness of God in Him*" (2 Cor. 5:21).

It is on the merit of Jesus Christ alone that we are able to come confidently before the throne of God. Because of what He has done on the cross, our access to God is guaranteed. What an incredible privilege, and what an incredible gift! However, we must always keep in mind how that access was purchased. It is because of what Jesus has done that we can come before God boldly. The word *boldness* has some interesting meanings—it means "to be frank, blunt, to be given freedom to speak unreservedly." The picture here is that of a soldier approaching a superior officer and asking for permission to speak freely. God has given us permission to be blunt and frank in our praying to Him.

Many would confuse the instruction to be bold with "be *demanding*." Make no mistake, you and I are in no position to demand anything of God. We are to *ask!* There is nothing wrong, however, with being unreserved in our asking, persistent in our asking, or even specific in our asking.

There is also nothing wrong with taking the promises of the Lord and asking Him to honor them. They are His promises, and we are not being presumptuous in asking Him to come through on what He has said. Praying Scripture is one way to pray with boldness. For example, take a promise like Psalm 50:15: *"Call upon Me in the day of trouble; I shall rescue you, and you will honor Me."* On multiple occasions, during some extremely difficult days, I have quoted this Scripture in prayer and clung to it fiercely. I have not been shy or reserved in reminding God of what He said. True to the Scripture, God has rescued and delivered my family and me on those occasions, and in return, it has been our joy to honor Him and testify of His never-ending faithfulness.

I hold in my heart some things that I believe the Lord has called me to trust Him for. I am bold in asking for those things, because I believe they are His desire for me. If I know He already wants me to have those things, I have greater confidence to be bold in my prayers. You see, we all need help to navigate the seas and storms of life. As we come into His presence, we find grace, lovingkindness, and favor with Him—who doesn't need that? *I* need God's lovingkindness and favor. If He only gave us what we deserve, we would come up empty-handed every time. Praise the Lord for grace even in our praying! Thank Him for favor and lovingkindness when we deserve a deaf ear to all our requests.

Grace in praying means God giving us what we could not earn or deserve. This was brought home once again to me this morning after a prayer time in which I was asking the Lord to bless my family. I did not specify what *type* of blessing but left that to His discretion. Later, I received a phone call from one of our church members, letting me know that she and her husband are going to give my family a quarter of a side of beef and are planning to do the same thing for our youth and worship minister. Now, my family does not deserve that blessing; that is God's grace in praying. Though I did not specify the blessing I was seeking, I was bold in my asking the Lord to bless my family, and He did, in a real and concrete way.

By the very fact that we stumble into the presence of the Lord, we are admitting our dependence on Him; we are facing the fact that we need God. There are multiple situations in life where we just cannot pull ourselves up by our own boot straps. There are countless times when our wisdom does not provide the solution to the problem and we need God to provide answers.

Many people live their whole lives without acknowledging that they need God. They trudge ahead alone and in their own finite strength. Over the years, life beats them down, and they usually end up broken, miserable people. They lose heart and hope. Sooner or later we all face things we cannot fix or overcome on our own, like sickness, death, accidents, or tragedy. But the Christian who prays may face all the same things and yet still find joy, hope, and peace before the throne of grace. Christians should never be too proud to come before their Father and just ask for help.

I see this principle at work in my boys. I will watch them work hard and become increasingly frustrated when they cannot untangle a knot in a shoelace, open a jar, or reach something above their heads. Many times I just sit back and wait for them to ask; I do not intervene until they ask me to. I want them to realize that at times they are dependent on me and need my help. Those are great teaching opportunities, to show them that we must depend on God to help us through the difficult times in life. There are burdens too heavy for us to lift, problems we cannot solve, decisions we do not have the wisdom to make, and sorrows too difficult to endure without divine help.

There are times when I cannot reach the answer even when I get on my tiptoes, and, therefore, I am forced to ask the Lord for help. We are independent by nature, but independence and self-reliance are not character traits highly honored by God. We would rather stretch our fingers to the max, on our tiptoes on the top rung of a ladder, trying to reach something God keeps just out of our grasp. Yet our God desires to be wanted and approached for help.

Therefore, we are to *ask* for help confidently and boldly, and God will intervene in response to our asking. Next, we learn to *trust* Him more and to be more dependent. God is glorified—it is that simple. Bold prayer plus God's grace plus our dependence for help equals God's glorification through answers.

Let me conclude this chapter with an illustration about praying boldly. Several years ago the Lord allowed me to go to Cuba on a mission trip. It was the first time I had ever left the United States. While flying there I prayed what I thought was a bold prayer; I asked the Lord to save fifty people through my preaching and ministry that week. I was scheduled to preach half a dozen times while I was there.

I was somewhat overwhelmed when I learned upon arriving in Havana that each person on the team would be dropped off in a city and left there alone for seven days with a Cuban host family. I was understandably nervous, because I do not speak any Spanish, but fortunately the pastor in whose home I stayed spoke a little English. It was often frustrating trying to communicate with each other, but we managed to converse through broken English and body language. I was assigned to the town of Guines, Cuba, which has some 80,000 people and very few Protestant churches.

Men like Samuel Reyes even pastor three different churches at the same time while making less than $10 a month.

The poverty in Cuba was beyond anything I had ever seen before. Very few people owned cars, and I actually saw several people traveling by horse and buggy. Most people either walked or rode bicycles, like the family I saw riding one bike together—the father pedaled, the mother rode on the handlebars, and a little girl around three years old rode on the back fender, clinging to her daddy. I could not believe the things I saw during that week—some people even drove tractors for transportation.

The preaching started off slowly, since it was the first time I had ever had to preach with an interpreter. Gradually, my interpreter, Helen, and I began to adjust to each other as I preached the gospel to the people of Cuba, which was my one aim that week—to preach the gospel to the lost and see fifty people saved. Helen, an English teacher, invited me to preach to her class, which ranged from teenagers to middle-age adults, all gathered to study English in a makeshift classroom in Helen's home. I was thrilled when several people accepted Christ, including twin girls in their twenties. The next day I preached at the First Baptist Church of Guines, a modest church building with a little over 100 in attendance. More people were saved during that service and at the other service I was able to preach at the church.

Later in the week, I was taken to preach in a dilapidated church building on the other side of Guines. The building was so decrepit that I could actually see the stars through the boards forming the walls of the church. I heard later that people in the community were afraid to even enter the building for fear of it collapsing on them. That tiny wreck of a building could barely hold fifty people, but I preached the gospel the best I could that night, trusting God to bridge the language and cultural barriers through my interpreter, Helen. Many responded to Christ that week, but I was greatly discouraged when I did a mental tally and discovered that we had seen a total of thirty-seven people saved. I rejoiced in every soul saved, but I been bold in asking God to save *fifty*. So I walked back to my host home after that last sermon a little disappointed that the Lord had not fully answered my prayers.

A van was to arrive around lunch the next day to take me back to the capital, Havana, where I was to join the rest of the team. On the walk back from the tiny church, however, Helen asked if I would be willing to preach one last time to a different English class in her home the next morning. I jumped at the chance and began asking God to save an additional thirteen souls.

Pastor Samuel and I hurried off to Helen's home early the next morning. We had to walk briskly to get there so I would not miss my ride to Havana later. I preached the love of Christ as simply as I knew how and offered each student in that class the hope of eternal life. I asked all who wanted to trust Christ for salvation to raise their hands as Helen translated my impassioned plea to them. Hands went up all over the room. There were mothers, fathers, and teenagers— all with their hands raised. I began counting...one, two, three...nine, ten, eleven, twelve. I did the math in my head: thirty-seven plus twelve equals forty-nine. *Forty-nine*. I could not believe we had come so close and I had missed the thing I had been boldly asking for—by *one* person.

Pastor Samuel had been standing in the doorway near the sidewalk while I was preaching and was trying to get my attention. When I finally noticed him, he pointed to a woman out on the sidewalk who been walking by, heard me preaching and stopped to listen, and was standing there outside the room with her hand lifted high in front of the whole community, indicating that she too had prayed to receive Christ. *Hallelujah*! She made the *fiftieth* person saved in that town during the week. I had a picture taken with her before she walked on, and then Pastor Samuel and I hurried back to catch my van.

How could I ask God for fifty souls? I knew it was God's will to save souls, so I could pray confidently. I asked for fifty because I knew that number was beyond my ability, especially with the language barrier. In the United States, if fifty people are saved in a revival meeting, that is a big deal. You seldom hear of an occasion like that, and I certainly had never seen anything like it in the years of my travels proclaiming the gospel.

God saving that woman out on the sidewalk once again showed me His power. That was such a dramatic experience that only *God* could have orchestrated it, and as a result, He got all the glory. Once again, God gave me a front-row seat to behold His faithfulness. As a result, I am more determined than ever to pray with boldness and to believe Him for the impossible. That is why I continually come before His throne to ask for things with boldness.

CHAPTER 9

Taking God at His Word

"If you abide in Me, and My words abide in you, ask whatever you wish, and it will be done for you. My Father is glorified by this, that you bear much fruit, and so prove to be My disciples" (John 15:7-8).

I was taking a seminary class on the gospel of John some time ago when the professor began lecturing on these two verses. He explained to the class that these verses were not literally true, that God in essence was not saying that when we ask whatever we wish we should expect that our wishes will be granted. He continued to make his point for a good season, and the longer he talked the more upset I became. One of our assignments for that class was to write a synopsis after each lecture and to identify any points of disagreement with the professor. Did I ever disagree with *this* lecture! I took several pages to tell him so and to explain why I believed what I believe.

Why are we so quick to explain away the promises of God? Why do we make excuses concerning God's promises, trying to convince ourselves and others that God does not really mean what His Word says? Does God mean what He says or not?

I will be the first to agree that there are certainly verses that I do not believe God wants us to take literally. For example, did Jesus mean for us to literally follow His commands when He said this?

> *"If your right eye makes you stumble, tear it out and throw it from you; for it is better for you to lose one of the parts of your body, than for your whole body to be thrown into hell. If your right hand makes you stumble, cut it off and throw it from you; for it is better for you to lose one of the parts of your body, than for your whole body to go into hell"* (Matt. 5:29-30).

As I look out over my congregation each Sunday morning, I do not see many one-eyed believers sitting in the pews or many with empty sleeves where their right hands should be. Yet there can be no doubt that every church is filled with normal human beings who constantly make mistakes. I remember as a young child picking up the Bible, taking it to my room, and reading it. I was lost at the time and had very little church background, but I knew that the words written in red were the words of Jesus. Somehow I stumbled across these two verses...and I was horrified! I may have been a little child, but I knew that my eye and hand had often caused me to stumble and sin. I was scared that Jesus really expected me to pluck out my eye and chop off my right hand! Soon after that my best friend came over, and I took him into my bedroom, sat him on the floor, and showed him those verses. We both sat there scared out of our wits, thinking we had found some secret verses no one else knew about and that it was our job to keep them a secret so we could still have our eyes and hands to play ball. We may chuckle at a story like that, but little children take things at face value.

As adults, we realize that Jesus is making a point about not letting anything in our lives stand in the way of trusting Christ for salvation or allowing sin to have dominion over us. But why is it that when we read a verse like John 15:7 we are so quick to dismiss its literal meaning? We use our critical thinking skills and deduce that Jesus could not really mean what that verse says, on several levels. First, not every wish is a wish that honors Him. Second, we do not really know anyone who has claimed a verse like that in prayer and has seen any tangible evidence of that verse being literally true. Third, if that verse were meant to be taken literally, it would be the talk of the Church. You would be able to *see* tangible evidence—the proof of the promise.

If John 15:7 were really true, why do we not hear it talked about in our religious circles like *The Prayer of Jabez* was? Why does it remain buried in the fifteenth chapter of the gospel of John?—a gospel that gets lots of attention, mind you, but this verse seems to be seldom commented on. It is almost like the Church reads this verse sleepily and yawns, "God does not really mean that!"

Why *doesn't* God mean that? I'm telling you, I believe that verse is to be taken literally and that if the Church really did so, the results would be dramatic.

The reason we don't see God honoring that verse in many people's lives is because, like many other promises, it is conditional. Psalm 37:4 is another conditional promise: *"Delight yourself in the LORD; And He will give you the desires of your heart."* The condition precedes the promise. The condition in this verse is that we must first delight ourselves in the Lord. He must be our chief joy and treasure; He must be the prize we seek above any other prize He could bestow on us in response to prayer. When we delight in Him this much, He says He will bless us with the desires of our hearts.

I have been living this verse for years. I married the woman I wanted to marry. I have been blessed with four boys of my own and a wonderful adopted daughter in Jennifer, Brenda's youngest sister, who came to live with us when she was in eighth grade. I love my calling to be a pastor and to serve the flock in FBC Paradise. God is granting me all the desires of my heart in a place to serve.

Let me give you just one small illustration of what kind of church I serve and how I feel that God's calling for us to move here is such an answer to prayer. This past Sunday we added a second morning worship service to our Sunday program. In addition to our evening service and a men's study I lead on Sunday afternoons, the two morning services keep my plate pretty full. I used to also meet with some men to pray early on Monday mornings, and so between my responsibilities on Sunday and Monday I was pretty fatigued.

This past Monday, one of our regular attendees was a little late for prayer meeting and came in looking exhausted. When I made mention of it he told me he had been at a nursing home sitting with the son of an elderly church member who is near death. This man told the son that since I was leaving for a praying and writing retreat the next morning he did not want to call me and disturb me, and he stayed with that family himself until 1:30 in the morning. When he told me that—with no praise for himself—I felt all over again that God had given me the desires of my heart in this church. It welled up deep within me to ask the Lord for a long ministry in Paradise. I know that it is not up to me, but it is the sincere desire of my heart.

113

Once the condition is met on the front end of God's promises, He is faithful to keep the back end—even in John 15:7. We can take God at His word if we are willing to keep the conditions on the front end. So what are the conditions of John 15:7? Jesus said, *"If you abide in Me, and My words abide in you..."* The two conditions here are plain: the first is that we must abide in Christ, and the second is that His words must abide in us.

What does it mean for a person to abide in Christ? Hudson Taylor, a missionary to China and the founder of the China Inland Mission, called this the "hidden life" or the "exchanged life." Literally, the life of Christ is exchanged for our lives when we hide ourselves in Him, so much so that Christ's nature is reflected and not our own. This is not an easy condition to meet—our fleshly natures are diametrically opposed to it. Galatians 5:17 says, *"For the flesh sets its desire against the Spirit, and the Spirit against the flesh; for these are in opposition to one another, so that you may not do the things you that please."* The flesh does not *want* to be hidden in Christ or to be exchanged for the spirit life, and it will not yield one square inch of territory without a life and death struggle. Interestingly, that is exactly what it will take to learn to *abide*, or to dwell and remain, in Christ: it will take continual death blows to our flesh. Read what Paul had to say about this: *"I have been crucified with Christ; and it is no longer I who live, but Christ lives in me; and the life which I now live in the flesh I live by faith in the Son of God, who loved me and gave Himself up for me"* (Gal. 2:20). Did you notice what Paul said about the hidden or exchanged life? He said, *"The life which I now live in the flesh I live by faith in the Son of God."*

Through faith Paul became hidden in Christ by allowing the Spirit to crucify his flesh. This is not a pleasant experience. Paul had to learn to die to his will, his desires, his selfish ambitions, his comfort, his dreams, and his control of his future. The dream God had for Paul's life was one filled with pain and suffering. Acts 9:15-16 tells us, *"But the Lord said to him; 'Go, for he is a chosen instrument of Mine, to bear My name before the Gentiles and kings and the sons of Israel; for I will show him how much he must suffer for My name's sake.'"*

Through his symbolic crucifixion with Christ, Paul learned to be hidden in Christ. Paul's identity became swallowed up in the identity of Christ. He learned to dwell in Christ, and regardless of suffering, Paul would write,

> *But whatever things were gain to me, those things I have counted as loss for the sake of Christ. More than that, I count all things to be loss in view of the surpassing value of knowing Christ Jesus my Lord, for whom I have suffered the loss of all things, and count them but rubbish so that I may gain Christ* (Phil. 3:7-8).

Christ was of infinite more value to Paul than anything the world could afford him.

For Paul, abiding in Christ meant not only being crucified with Christ but also treasuring and valuing Christ above everything, including earthly comfort. When you and I can get to that point, we will know we are learning how to abide in Christ and will begin to experience the exchanged life.

I read a story about Watchman Nee, a pastor and author from China, that really illustrates what it means to abide in Christ. One day Nee was being falsely accused by a brother in the faith. Eyewitnesses said that Nee determined that he would not defend himself to this angry brother but would remain hidden in Christ. For three straight hours Nee was berated and bashed, his integrity questioned and his character assassinated, and all the while he never uttered one single word in defense.

I know how many times I have been quick to defend myself in similar situations, only showing that I have a long way to go before I truly learn what it means to abide in Christ. Abiding in Christ means *continual communion* with Christ, just like a branch remains connected to and communes with the tree. As long as the branch remains connected to the tree, it really does not have any separate identity but is considered a part of the tree itself. As long as the branch remains part of the tree, there is life, but once the branch breaks off and becomes independent of the tree, nourishment stops and death soon follows. This explains why most of us cannot take God at His word in John 15:7. The breakdown in this promise occurs when we are not able to abide in Christ, but there is no breakdown on God's behalf. He is more than willing to meet His end of the promise, but we make excuses and continue to live without the intended power and blessing of God.

We are selfish with our lives; we like our own identities. I recall talking to a young minister several years ago who told me he was ready to "get busy" in ministry. He wanted to get out and make a name for himself. I quickly reminded him that his purpose as a minister was to be exalting the name of Christ; *his* name was irrelevant.

If you want to take God at His Word in this verse, are you willing to learn to abide in Christ? I predict it to be a long, difficult, but incredibly rewarding journey for any who decide to meet this condition in John 15:7. Living the exchanged life may require much sacrifice. Let me give you one example. As I have sought to learn to abide in Christ, I have realized that He has the right to get me up at whatever time He wants to for prayer. As a result, I have not slept with an alarm clock in over a decade. This week has been unusual, but the Lord has awakened me at 3:30 one morning, 4:00 the next, 4:30 the day after that, and at 5:30 this morning. It hurts my flesh to get up so early and then try to maintain the normal duties of the day. The spirit in me is willing, but the flesh battles against the spirit and there have been many times when I loved sleep more than I loved fellowship with the Father.

Besides abiding in Christ, there is also a second condition to be met if we want God to do whatever we ask Him. Not only are *we* to abide in *Christ* but His *words* are to abide in *us*. Again, the word *abide* means "to remain, to dwell," and "to stay." How often do you frequent God's word for meditation and for guidance? The Psalmist writes,

> *How blessed is the man who does not walk in the counsel of the wicked, Nor stand in the path of sinners, Nor sit in the seat of scoffers! But his delight is in the law of the LORD, And in His law he meditates day and night* (Ps. 1:1-2).

> *My soul is crushed with longing After Your ordinances at all times* (Ps. 119:20).

> *O how I love Your law! It is my meditation all the day* (Ps. 119:97).

> *How sweet are Your words to my taste! Yes, sweeter than honey to my mouth!* (Ps. 119:103).

I rise before the dawn and cry for help; I wait for Your words. My eyes anticipate the night watches, That I may meditate on Your word" (Ps. 119:148).

There is a woman in our church who has this kind of heart for the Scriptures. She is amazing—she reads the Bible through at least three times, and sometimes four times, each year. The more she reads, the more she learns, and the more she learns, the better she prays. She is always eager to begin again and learn something new. God's Word truly abides in her soul; when she prays, she is most likely to pray in the will of God and pray the heart of God over a given situation. And that is the point—God wants us to pray for the things *He* desires. When our desires and God's desires become one, we can do some powerful praying, and we will be able to take God at His Word. The more we saturate ourselves in the Scriptures, the more we will know the mind and heart of God.

Having God's Word abide in your heart will take more than a five- or ten-minute pithy little devotional thought and Scripture reading. You will have to *linger* in the Word, meditate on the Word, ponder the Word, peruse the Word, read the Word, and muse with God over His law. When His Word really begins to sink in, when Scriptures surface in real-life situations without great effort, when you bleed Scripture in your thought life and conversations, then you will know that His Word really dwells and remains in you.

We have no shortage of Bible teaching, but we do have great shortages of Bible retention. A quick test: can you remember the text your pastor preached from this past Sunday? What about the Sunday before that? If you are struggling to remember, you are not alone. That is why diving deep into the Word *daily* is a must. The more we do this, the more we retain and the more His Word abides in us.

When you have come to the place where you are abiding in Him and His Word is abiding in you, get ready. Real fireworks can spark in your prayer life. That is why Jesus could say at the end of John 15:7, *"Ask whatever you wish [or will or desire], and it will be done for you."* That is why I can pray with boldness about our church in Paradise. I believe that I honestly want what God wants and that I am praying prayers that originated in His heart first. When that is the case, there is a guarantee that what we are asking God for will come to pass and become reality. *That* is taking God at His Word.

You and I may be ridiculed and misunderstood along the way for taking God at His Word. Let that be as it may. May we never make excuses for God's Word not being fulfilled in our lives. May we continue to pray extreme prayers birthed in the heart of God and revealed to us first through our abiding in Him and then through His Word abiding in us. May we always be men and women who do not shrink back from taking God at His Word. The results will be amazing. Imagine sitting around your living room in your old age surrounded by your children, their spouses, and all your grandchildren, giving testimony of all the times you took God at His Word and beheld His faithfulness. Your children and grandchildren will receive a great heritage of faith and continue to trust the Lord as they have seen modeled in your life.

> *For He established a testimony in Jacob And appointed a law in Israel, which He commanded our fathers That they should teach them to their children, That the generation to come might know, even the children yet to be*

119

born, That they may arise and tell them to their chil-
dren, That they should put their confidence in God
And not forget the works of God, But keep His com-
mandments (Ps. 78:5-7).

Don't settle for anything less than God's direct power
continually flowing through and around your life. May
prayer be a continual oasis pouring the love and blessings of
God from His throne to your life.

I have to end this chapter with a powerful story and illustration of this truth being lived out right before my very
eyes. Darrell and Charissa Fishbeck are ministry partners
with us here at FBC Paradise, and more than that, they are
friends. When they came to serve with us here over a year
ago, we learned of Charissa's great passion for horses, which
began when she was a little girl. In fact, it was her dream and
the desire of her heart to own her own horse one day. Since
Darrell and Charissa could not afford to buy one, Charissa
had long ago turned her request over to God and asked Him
to grant her the desire of her heart.

Years of prayers mixed with tears and confusion challenged Charissa. The dream in her heart was not only for a
horse but also for God to use that horse to bring glory to
His name through ministry. Her burden became my
burden; I often asked her about it, and she would many
times tear up as the thought of her dream and the pain of
not seeing it fulfilled would surface. Charissa battled her
emotions constantly, wondering whether the dream was
planted by God or if it was a selfish dream. It was not easy
living in Paradise where every day on her way to work or
church she drove past house after house with horses in the
pastures. I am sure there were days that she asked God why

she desired something so deeply that He would not allow her to have.

God's grace did put Charissa *around* horses. Her neighbors owned horses and from time to time granted her the joy of riding them and working with them. She was also put into contact with some people who put on foxhunts, an activity Charissa had never even imagined participating in. It was a thrilling day when she was invited to join a foxhunt and found herself falling in love with a whole new area of horsemanship. Little did she know that God was in the process of taking the desires of her heart, the tears she had prayed through, and her patient abiding in Christ to grant her a miracle beyond her wildest imagination.

Being around horses all the time intensified Charissa's desire to own her own horse and to somehow use it for God's glory. It seemed obvious to me that the Lord had created that passion for horses in her and wanted to bless it. As I prayed with her about getting a miracle horse, I became convinced that it was God's will for her have one, but I knew that, like everything else in our spiritual journeys, it would have to take place in God's timing. Months and months of prayers ensued. I watched as Charissa went from unwavering faith to confusion about whether the desires of her heart were selfishly motivated. I watched as she died to her dream over and over again and learned to be content in her current circumstances. Only those who have trod that same soil know the pain and frustration of waiting on God. Much abiding in Christ and much prayer sustained Charissa, and what happened next is nothing short of a miracle.

One of the ladies Charissa had met on her foxhunts found out about some horses that were going to be slaughtered. This woman, Donna, was moved to go and rescue as many of them as she could at an auction. Two horses really caught her eye, but she had exceeded the amount of money that she and her husband had agreed she could spend. By the time she contacted her husband about saving the two horses and got his permission to proceed, the horses had been purchased and loaded on a trailer to be taken to a slaughterhouse near Houston.

Most people would have been disappointed but they would have given up, and that would have been where the story ended—but not Donna. She persistently followed that trailer all the way to Houston and bought the two horses she had spotted at the auction right off the trailer on the parking lot of the slaughterhouse. Days later, during the last foxhunt of the year, Donna told Charissa about her journey and that she'd be willing to sell one of the horses for exactly what she had paid for him—$600.

As Charissa listened to Donna's story, she commented, "If that were my horse I would name him Lazarus, for he has come back from the dead." She e-mailed the story to me, and the Lord captured my heart with it. I just knew that this was the miracle she had been asking for and that God would get a great amount of glory through the horse named Lazarus. I e-mailed Charissa back and challenged her to do something presumptuous—I challenged her to contact Donna and to tell her that she would have the $600 for her within two weeks. Charissa took a huge leap of faith and made the offer, even though she and Darrell did not have the $600. Brenda and I did not have $600 either, but we began praying for it so we could give it to them. That same night when I was with our Monday night prayer warriors, I told them this story and together we asked the Lord for $600 for Charissa's horse.

Our church was going through *Experiencing God* at this time, and God had been using the study in many lives in profound ways. Thanks to that study, Charissa experienced God in a way that was both personal and awe-inspiring. She was working through her study one evening when she read the following statement: "If you have experienced the silences of God, briefly describe one such time below." Charissa immediately thought of her dream to own her own horse and how the Lord had been silent for over two years. Her mind drifted off to the nearly exterminated horse she had affectionately named Lazarus. After some prayer and strict redirection of her thoughts, she moved on to the next part of the study. What she read next was the loving, gentle voice of God speaking to His daughter. As she describes it, it made projectile tears shoot from her eyes. Here is what she read:

> One morning I was reading the story of Lazarus (John 11:1-45). Let me go through the sequence of what happened as I read: John reported that Jesus loved Lazarus, Mary, and Martha. Having received word that Lazarus was sick unto death, Jesus delayed going until Lazarus died. In other words, Mary and Martha asked Jesus to come help their brother, and there was silence. All the way through the final sickness and death of Lazarus, Jesus did not respond. They received no response from the One who said He loved Lazarus. Jesus even said He loved Mary and Martha. Yet, there was still no response.
>
> Lazarus died. They went through the entire funeral process. They fixed his body, put him in the grave, and covered it with a stone. Still they experienced silence from God. Then Jesus said to the disciples,

"Let's go." When Jesus arrived, Lazarus had been dead four days. Martha said to Jesus, "Lord, if you had been here, my brother would not have died."

Then the Spirit of God began to help me understand something. It seemed to me as if Jesus had said to Mary and Martha; "You are exactly right. If I had come, your brother would not have died. You know that I could have healed him, because you have seen me heal many, many times. If I had come when you asked me to, I would have healed him. But, you would have never known any more about Me than you already know. I knew that you were ready for a greater revelation of Me than you have ever known in your life. I wanted you to come to know that I am the resurrection and the life. My refusal and My silence were not rejection. It was an opportunity for Me to disclose to you more of Me than you have ever known."[6]

Charissa was stunned, believing that reading about Lazarus in the course of her *Experiencing God* study was not coincidence. I agreed. The following morning, Darrell found an envelope with $600 that had been slipped under his office door, with a note in it instructing them to go and buy Charissa's horse. By that time, Donna had come down on the price and even at one point offered the horse for free, but Charissa felt deeply that God had made the provision and the full amount should be paid. It would take another book to discuss how the Lord used all of this in Donna's heart and the hearts of those who went through it with Charissa.

---

[6] Henry Blackaby, *Experiencing God* (Nashville: Lifeway Church Resources, 1990), p. 93-94.

Today, Charissa no longer owns Lazarus but is reminded of the giving, her long-awaited dream from a loving Father who remained silent for such a long time only so she could come to know Him in a way she had never known Him before. Lazarus has already brought much glory to God. I will not forget the following Wednesday night when she stood and testified before the church about what the Lord had done. We rejoiced and wept with her, and we spent the rest of that evening praying for people. There was even an article in the local newspaper about Lazarus, with a picture of Charissa and the horse. Her next-door neighbors gave her permission to keep Lazarus in their pasture and to have access to their horse facilities, and God made other provision by giving her a saddle, halter, and bridle.

Now I want you to read the Scriptures we have meditated on in this chapter. You tell me if we can take them literally as we take God at His Word: *"If you abide in Me, and My words abide in you, ask whatever you wish, and it will be done for you"* (John 15:7).

CHAPTER 10

Praying with Tenacity and Endurance

Now He was telling them a parable to show that at all times they ought to pray and not to lose heart (Luke 18:1).

Let us not lose heart in doing good, for in due time we will reap if we do not grow weary (Gal. 6:9).

I was called to preach when I was eighteen years old. It was the summer following my senior year in high school, and I was at a youth camp. When I made that call public at my church, people asked me if I was going to be a pastor or a youth minister, and I really did not know what to tell them. I did not know if God's call on my life meant that I would be a pastor, youth minister, or evangelist. All I knew was that God had called me to preach.

My pilgrimage in the ministry has been interesting. On more than one occasion I have been tempted to give up and walk away from it. I have even, on a couple of occasions in the midst of some dark valleys, picked up the want ads to look for other job opportunities. Over and over again, however, God has brought me back to His call on my life. Throughout the years since I first heard the call I have served as a youth minister, pastor, church planter, college minister, and full-time evangelist. To be honest, much of my ministry experience has been deeply painful and frustrating. In fact, until we moved to Paradise, most of our ministry labors produced very little. From the time God called me, I only had one prayer: "God, please use me." There were variations on that prayer, but for over twenty-one years that has been the constant cry of my heart. *"God, please use me. God, I want to be used in greater ways. God, how can you use me more?"* In hindsight, I can see that in the early years a lot of that praying was motivated by my own selfish ambition; I wanted to be in large churches preaching before grand crowds. God's solution was to keep me in smaller churches in out-of-the-way places for most of that time.

The second church where I served as youth minister was in Weatherford, Texas, and was a great experience up until the end. Yet, even then my selfish ambition was preeminent. My one goal was to have the largest youth group in town. We saw some amazing things, but eventually the whole youth group disintegrated right before my eyes because I was not laboring for the glory of God alone.

Selfish ambition remained high on the throne of my heart when I was called to be the pastor of the Burke Baptist Church. I saw myself in competition with other churches and coveted church growth awards for myself as much as for the Lord. Our church did grow in the beginning—Burke nearly doubled in attendance in about a year and a half—but just as quickly it began to decline.

I will never forget a denominational meeting we attended locally where our church was given an award for being the fastest-growing church in our area. I received no pleasure in walking to the front of the room to receive that award because I knew that back at the church people were bailing out right and left and we were on the verge of going through a split, much of it my fault. Attendance was dwindling, and that long-sought-after church growth award seemed empty and hollow in my hands as I walked back to my seat that day. That award felt like bitter water in my mouth, and I wanted to spew it out. The Lord used that experience to break me and purge me. For the last two years of my ministry at Burke, we ended up with a little over two dozen people in the church. It was a very painful time, and no matter what I did I could not understand why the Lord was not *using* me. People would tell me often that I was an anointed preacher, but nobody wanted to come to our church to listen.

Over the two years following our receiving that award, the Lord really began to teach me the difference between being a *preacher* and being a *pastor*. God took me through deep valleys in order to teach me how to be a shepherd and to show mercy and kindness to those who were hurting. My years at Burke Baptist Church were extremely painful, for the members and for me. I was young, naive, overconfident, and much in need of brokenness. And the more the Lord broke me, the greater my desire was for Him to use me. But the harder I prayed this prayer, the more the attendance in the church plummeted. I voluntarily took two different cuts in my salary because the finances had fallen into such disarray as we continued to lose giving church members.

Mornings I awoke early and begged God for more anointing. I pounded the doors of heaven with many tears, asking for the church to turn around and for God to bless our ministry, often staying up late into the night—but to no avail. I would often go into the sanctuary alone during the week and pour out my soul on the altar. Eventually I came to a point where I did not know what else to pray. I dreaded trying to preach on Sundays, with an empty and disillusioned heart and a shattered faith.

Month after month I prayed but did not see anything change as far as our attendance or finances. We actually had to meet outside on Sunday evenings for the better part of the summer because we could not afford to pay the electric bill to keep the air conditioning running all day. It was not a fun time whatsoever, but those blazing hot July evening services—when the temperatures hovered in the triple digits—were used by God to teach me character.

I felt stripped of my dignity. Unfounded rumors spread around the community about me. It felt as if my family and I were the objects of gossip among the townspeople, other pastors, and former church members, not only in our little community but all over the county. I hurt as deeply as I have ever hurt in my life, or at least up to that point.

Little did I know that God's character-cleansing program was just beginning. What I perceived as an open door to start No Compromise Ministries and leave the pain of being a pastor behind was only a graduate course in the school of brokenness. I remember saying to myself upon leaving Burke, "I will never pastor a church again. Ever!"

Traveling with No Compromise Ministries was exciting at first. My prayer life was really strengthened during those five years. We often saw God's miraculous provision, but just as often I sat at home for weeks on end because no one called and invited me to preach. The prayer for God to use me continued. Often I wept when no one was around because I saw so many others being used and I could not understand why God would not use *me* in more significant ways. When doors did open for ministry, they were mostly in small out-of-the-way churches with small crowds and small offerings. I determined to never make money an issue; I went anywhere I was invited, regardless of whether they could afford to pay me or not. I preached as hard to 20 as to 100 and to 100 as to 1,000.

My life was hard, and my friends often told me that they did not understand why God was not blessing our ministry. My self-confidence began to shrivel. It pained my heart to hear people tell me I was anointed, because I would always say to myself, "If I am really anointed, why doesn't God use me in greater ways?"

During the years of traveling with No Compromise Ministries, I saw the painful death of several dreams and felt public humiliation. I felt mandated by the Lord to start a citywide youth meeting once a month, called "The Revolution." Attendance was always small, and eventually interest in that ministry waned and died altogether. I was also a co-founder of a ministry called "Generation Xcellence," or GX, a weekly outreach for college students. It grew in the beginning, but eventually it too died a slow, painful death after several years of me pouring my heart and soul into the lives of those students. In the end it felt more like a social gathering than a worship time together.

Next I felt led to hold tent crusades. The first one was a bust, since it rained all week. I remember standing under the tent one afternoon as water flooded the tent, totally immersing all of the electrical chords. We had to move the meeting into a gymnasium, where attendance was small and no one was saved. Other plans for future crusades fell through the cracks and never really got off the ground. It was failure on top of failure, and I could not make sense out of any of it. I wanted so badly to be used for the Lord and to do something of significance in the kingdom of God, but instead of seeing ministry success I kept facing failures, one after another. During my full-time traveling years I saw many people saved, some real moves of God, and I know the Lord taught me how to really trust Him, but I never felt that the Lord was really blessing me and using me like I had asked Him to.

Suddenly there was a call on my life to start a church. Being confident that starting a church was what God had told us to do, Brenda and I chose the name CentrePointe Community Church. It began with a handful of college students in my home. We prayed, planned, knocked on doors, studied Scripture, and dreamed God's dream together. Eventually we had close to thirty people crammed into my living room for church on Sunday mornings. It was exciting, it was fresh and new, and I began to believe that all my frustrations and ministry plans had been preparing me to start that church. In my mind it all finally made sense, and hope began to surface that at long last God was going to really use me to do something significant for Him. During that time our driveway would have cars jammed in it, with others lining the streets on both sides. In those early days, we would rearrange the furniture in our living room early each Sunday morning and set out rows of chairs in anticipation of those who would join us. I really began to think that finally God was blessing something we felt called to do.

The people loved us, and the church really began to pick up momentum. We became the talk of the town, but other churches were jealous, and once again we found ourselves the subject of rumors. Though most of them were either totally unfounded or completely misinformed, these rumors eventually took a toll on us.

We found a building to lease and began to remodel it. For nearly a year we would sacrifice our Saturdays to work on that building, eventually completing the inside. (We never had the time or money to work on the outside.) We set our launch date and passed out invitations and door hangers. We had heating problems the week prior to the church opening, and it was nip and tuck to see if we were really going to make the first service. I was on the phone with people, getting last minute things fixed in the building, up until late Friday afternoon prior to our first Sunday service.

We went public, and the crowd increased. In a matter of only a few months we grew from thirty to about seventy. We saw people get saved, and I finally felt the Lord was honoring my prayer of over fifteen years to be used by Him in greater ways. I could not have foreseen the pain that was just around the corner.

Over the next year, our core people started leaving the church...one after another. The excitement of starting a new church sank into the spiritual and physical exhaustion of never-ending work and financial stress. Then we had a moral issue surface with a key leader in the church. The vision began to lose its luster, and before I knew it, I was sitting in a meeting with all of our key donors and financial supporters, who were telling me, "You gave it your best shot, but things are not turning around, and we believe it is time to pull the plug." Our denominational leaders said it, my very own pastor supported this decision, and as I was sitting in that meeting I could not disagree that God had ceased blessing the church. Our youth minister (and my long-term ministry partner with No Compromise) accepted a call to serve as a youth pastor to a large church in San Angelo, and I was left alone to sort out the pain of my shattered dreams. All I could think was that once again I had failed. I trusted God, had given Him all I had, and still the dream died—and so did my hope and belief that the Lord would ever really allow me to be successful in ministry. In essence, as CentrePointe slowly died, something in me died as well.

On December 7, 2003, I stood before the dozen or so people who were left in our church and told them that the dream was over. I had no salary, no place to minister, and no hope. There were some who did not agree, but I was not open to beating my head against the wall, trying to breathe life into something that God was obviously not blessing.

That was when I came to this same prayer cabin I am writing this in right now to seek direction from the Lord about what to do next. While on that prayer retreat I sensed the Lord say clearly, "Do not get a secular job. Trust Me, and do not ask anyone for money." In my thinking, God was going to quickly open a door for another church to call me as their pastor.

Resumes were sent out to several churches, and we prayed and waited. I knew I could trust the Lord to take care of us for a couple of months until another ministry door opened. But doors that should have opened slammed in our faces, leaving us baffled and disillusioned. We interviewed with a church in Tyler in which I had preached several times while traveling in full-time evangelism. We knew many of the people on the search committee—even the parents of some dear friends. So when the door was shut, we couldn't believe it. What we didn't know then was that this was only the first of what turned out to be thirty-two churches that would officially reject me as pastor. With each rejection came sorrow like a dagger into my heart and my faith like I have never known. Deep depression set in.

My prayer to be used by the Lord continued, but with less faith. Some of the CentrePointe people approached us after a couple of months about meeting in our home again for Bible study because they had not been able to find a church and we had no place to go either. Every church we visited was another blow to my dignity. This lasted for over a year, and Sunday after Sunday about half a dozen adults would show up in my living room for Bible study and to sing with the accompaniment of an acoustic guitar. I continually wrestled with wondering whether the Lord wanted to bless CentrePointe and turn the church around or whether we were released and needed to move on to another church.

I will never forget the lowest point of my entire ministry—the Sunday when only one woman showed up for worship. Brenda was in our bedroom teaching Sunday school to our boys and her boys, and that woman and I were left alone in our living room. I wanted to cry but forced myself to teach her the truth of God's Word. It was awkward for both us, and when she left, I hit a wall emotionally. My reasoning went, "God, You called me to preach, but You will not let me preach. I sit in a chair in my living room and teach Your Word faithfully, and I have persevered with crowds of six or less. I even taught one today! I have asked You to use me, but You continue not to. Why did You place a call on my life if You are not going to use me? You are not blessing CentrePointe, and You will not open a door for us to leave. You told me not to get a job but to trust You. I do not understand why You are afflicting me this way."

My mood swings went from times of great faith to times of dark, dark depression. As a family, we saw miracles that are still hard to believe in hindsight. Yet all I wanted was to give up. I questioned why God had ever called me into the ministry. There were days when I would get in my car and drive around Loop 287 outside Lufkin and cry like a baby. The pain was raw and deep, and I didn't want Brenda to see me crack, because I knew she was struggling to trust God as well. I felt I had to be strong for her and the boys.

I began meditating on the book of Job a great deal. Finally, I had a breakthrough—I came to a place where I told the Lord I was willing to stay at CentrePointe forever and to live the remainder of my life without a salary. I surrendered my desire to be used in large churches and felt that God's lot for me was to remain in smaller churches for the rest of my ministry. I think Paul came to that same place as well when he wrote,

> *Not that I speak from want, for I have learned to be content in whatever circumstances I am. I know how to get along with humble means, and I also know how to live in prosperity; in any and every circumstance I have learned the secret of being filled and going hungry, both of having abundance and suffering need. I can do all things through Him who strengthens me* (Phil. 4:11-13).

God brought me to a place where I was set free from what people thought. Many people doubted that I ever heard God tell me not to get a job and to live by extreme faith. I ignored them and clung to God in prayer. I continued to pray and was determined to show a watching world that God does indeed answer prayer and that He alone is sufficient to meet any and every need we have.

CentrePointe fluctuated in attendance from around a dozen to a couple of dozen at times. We loved the people, and they loved us. We focused on the Word and prayed a great deal, but still I prayed privately for the Lord to do something significant with us. It was a continual pain in my heart, only by this time my selfish ambition had faded into the ambition to serve Christ. I longed to be used but longed *more* to obey and follow God for His glory.

During that season God stripped away my preaching behind a pulpit; I sat in a chair to teach for eighteen months. God took away my transportation when my car broke down while driving back from San Angelo, where I had preached the night before. God took away my salary, forcing me to trust Him to meet my every need. God took away dear and precious people who never returned to CentrePointe. God took away my ego as I had to honestly report how small our church was to people who asked.

During this time, Brenda and I discussed the possibility of traveling full-time again and moving to the Dallas–Fort Worth metroplex to be near her family. Some doors opened here and there for me preach at revivals and youth events around Texas, yet Brenda and I felt a deep sense of calling for me to serve as a pastor. I did not have a peace about taking up No Compromise Ministries full-time again. Pastoring a church was the call on my life (even though at one time I said I would never do it again).

I prayed. I taught the Word. I witnessed to lost men. I served the community and the school with a small band of less than one dozen members. I didn't like our circumstances, but I learned to be content in them. I learned to trust God and to behold His faithfulness time and time again.

Like the time we drove up in our driveway and noticed something hanging on our front doorknob. Inside the bag was a check for a little over $300. Only God could have done that. On another occasion we found a card wedged in our front door with a check for over $500 from people we had had no contact with for over three years. God continued to show us His faithfulness time and time again, and each time our faith became stronger and we learned to trust Him more. God truly honored His word in commanding me to not get a secular job and never to ask anyone for money but to trust Him.

That is not to say that there were not some seasons when we doubted and thought about throwing in the towel. I can think of two such incidents. The first couple of months of living without a salary were not that tough, but the third and fourth months were extremely difficult. The bills continued to mount while God's provision continued to dwindle, and we were facing serious trouble. I prayed and prayed and prayed. Daily I walked the twenty-six steps from my front door to our mailbox, believing for a miracle that did not come. No Compromise Ministries had a post office box that was about six miles from our house; I would drive to that post office in prayer, hoping for a miracle, but leave empty-handed and dejected. My friends kept telling me that I needed to get a job and provide for my family. I was very tempted to listen to them, but then God would remind me of His command to not get a job but to trust Him. There was a continual tug of war in my soul between logic and faith.

And then, in the middle of the fourth month of our "extreme faith adventure," God showed up in a dramatic way. I was helping a friend remodel his house when my cell phone rang. It was a pastor friend, telling me that someone had direct-deposited $4,000 into our checking account. How do you explain that? That is *not* something we could ever have foreseen or predicted. Not only did God prove to be our provider over and over again, we also were allowed to witness the creativity of God.

Go back to Luke 18:1: *"Now He was telling them a parable to show them that at all times they ought to pray and not to lose heart."* Each time we were up against the wall, God would come through and we would behold the faithfulness of God in renewing our faith. And not long after this huge miracle God did something else even more amazing. Part of our financial struggle included trying to make a house payment each month. We wrestled with selling the house, but in the end we felt the Lord leading us to trust Him for our house as well.

Thinking "logically," I put a "For Sale" sign in our front yard. One Saturday morning I was up early, praying in my converted bedroom office. While meeting with the Lord He asked me if I *really* trusted Him with my house. I had no steady income, and the payments had been a struggle even when I *did* have a salary, so trusting God with those house payments was a huge effort for me. But God wanted my absolute, total dependence and to show all of us how powerful He really is. I trapsed through the dew-dampened grass to take the "For Sale" sign out of the yard as proof of my trust in Him.

About a week after the $4,000 miracle, I was visiting a woman who was a faithful supporter of our ministry. I was recounting what the Lord had spoken to me about trusting Him and how God had provided for us. As I was leaving her office she walked outside with me, and what she said next was absolutely stunning: "Matt, God has told me to pay your house payment. I am going to pay it each month until God tells me to stop."

I looked at her and responded by telling her she could not do that, but I will never forget what she said next: "Shut up! This is not about you. This is about God!" That woman paid our house payment for the next *fifteen months* until the Lord moved us, without ever holding it over our heads. I have told that story over and over again to encourage those people who are at the end of their ropes and are ready to give up. *Don't give up! Never give up!* The same God who responded to my prayers in the eleventh hour will respond to your faith-filled, persevering, and tenacious prayers as well. *Never* quit praying or believing.

I know there are nights of weeping, but as Psalm 30:5 says, joy will come in the morning. Cling to God's Word, believe Him, and take His Word at face value no matter how long you have to wait or how difficult things become. Stay the course. Hang tough in your belief and refuse to let go. When you endure, your prayers will be answered.

As I have noted several times in this book already, God released us from East Texas and the CentrePointe Community Church. He planted us at the First Baptist Church of Paradise, and then He quadrupled attendance in our church in a little over eight months. God has finally begun honoring that twenty-year-long prayer for Him to use me significantly. I see all the pain and trials as being used to prepare me for such a time as this. The Lord helped me to not grow weary in doing good, and He is allowing us to reap a harvest as a result.

I'm not writing this book to get rich or to get my name in the spotlight. I am writing this book for the thousands of believers and pastors who are about to give up. My cry to you is to endure, continue to believe, hang in there, stay the course, *keep praying* and *trusting*. God will show Himself faithful on your behalf, just as He has done for me. I am having the time of my life in Paradise, where finally, after over a decade of waiting and trusting, I am seeing my ministry dreams come true. It has been worth the wait.

Looking back, it all makes sense: all the hundreds of hours spent praying, all the tears, all the days of depression overcome with continual reading of Scripture. All the early morning quiet times and late night prayer watches. It has all been worth it to get to experience what the Lord is allowing me to experience now. After beholding His faithfulness countless times, I can speak from experience: *gut it out.* Determine to press on in prayer until you get whatever you are believing Him to give.

The other day I was walking from my office to another part of the church building. I began looking at our recently remodeled stage, praise banners recently bought and hung, our new baby grand piano bought and paid for, and I was overwhelmed with gratitude. I had a worship experience in that place, all alone. "God, I don't know why You chose me. I do not deserve what You are doing right now. I am humbled by Your blessings, but I want to thank You for appointing me to this church. Thank You for the favor you have shown me with these people and this community. Thank You for calling me to be the pastor of this church."

By God's grace I persevered in prayer, and after two decades, God is finally allowing me to be used to do things I have long dreamed about and asked Him for. I am more humbled than ever, especially as He unfolds the future. He deserves all the credit and all the glory.

I know there are times when you think that God will never come through for you. I know that prolonged times of waiting can lead to doubt and discouragement. As you can see, I am just like you and have walked some of the same trails you currently find yourself walking. Please listen to this, fellow pilgrim: persevering prayer, *enduring* prayer, can see you through. You may hurt for a long while. You may waver in your faith. Keep feeding yourself the promises of God in Scripture and refuse to give up. I promise that God will come through for you as my family has seen Him come through for us time and time again. There is more faithfulness for all of us to behold.

CHAPTER 11

Praying that Accomplishes Much

Therefore confess your sins to one another, and pray for one another so that you may be healed. The effective prayer of a righteous man can accomplish much (Jas. 5:16).

What are the two desired results of prayer? One, that God would get more glory. Two, that we would see our prayers answered. Much takes place in our personal lives in between those two desired results: faith is strengthened, burdens are lifted, peace is gained, and we are brought into closer communion with God.

I just arose from my knees from praying with a fellow brother and warrior in this fight of faith. Our hearts were poured out to the Lord like water from a glass. It was one of the highlights of this entire praying and writing break I have been kindly afforded by the gracious people at FBC Paradise, and I do not take these cherished days for granted.

I recall in the middle of our supplications asking myself if I was going to play games in prayer or if I was really going to tenaciously go after answers by faith. I determined to secure answers and rose from my knees to lay hands on my brother and to pray for God to give birth to all the dreams this man has carried in his heart for decades. I prayed that the Lord would bless His dreams and show Him favor and success.

Then I began praying for my dreams, one of which is the publication of my books. I have asked the Lord to publish all of my books and for them to be distributed all over the world as He sees fit. I continually ask the Lord to allow my books to stand the test of time and to give them great kingdom impact. I am not now and never have been concerned with making money from my writing; rather, I want my books to leave deep imprints in the sands of people's lives for the glory of God. If I never make a penny from these books, I will still write, because He has called me to do so. In fact, we have given away more books as a ministry than we have ever sold and are delighted to be in a position to be able to do that.

However, I have been tempted to walk away from writing. Back in Lufkin I watched my books sit on shelves for weeks and months in local Christian bookstores without anyone buying them, which was very disheartening. Often I would find myself stopping by the two different Christian bookstores just to see if anyone had purchased a book, and 99 percent of the time no one had. It was not that I wanted to make money off the sales of those books. I longed for people to be blessed by them and for God to grow His kingdom in the hearts of people through those pages. I thought to myself, What good is music if nobody ever gets to hear it? What good is art if no one ever gets to view it? What good is a book sitting on a shelf if no one ever picks it up and reads it?

But something has happened in my soul this week while on this retreat. I am reassured that writing is a call on my life just like preaching is a call on my life. I asked God to see my books not only published but on the shelves of a mainline bookstore in the Dallas–Fort Worth metroplex and beyond. You see, I want to pray prayers that accomplish much, and one way is to see tangible results in my praying. Therefore I prayed a measurable prayer, and I believe that one day you will be able to walk into that chain of bookstores and see this book and others printed on the shelves—not to make much out of my name but to make much of God.

Very little of the praying in the body of Christ accomplishes much. For all our praying both inside and outside the church walls, we have little to show for it much of the time. What would happen if we really began to take some of these principles seriously? What would happen if we could learn to pray with great expectation, and the Lord answered our prayers in a mighty way? We would be even more motivated to pray. The power of God would be on display week after week. Pews would be packed, baptisteries would be in continuous use week after week, and our land would be revived.

Prayer ought to be as natural to us as breathing. We ought to expect answers. In fact, it should bother us when we pray and do *not* see answers. In those moments, we must discern if we are praying amiss and out of the will of God. Accomplishing much for the glory of the Lord should always be our aim.

Yesterday afternoon I was prostrate before the Lord praying for an elderly woman in our church who is near death. This woman's son has honored his mother every step of the way with his continual vigil at her side, and I prayed for him as well. As I prayed, I was interrupted by a phone call from one our church members telling me that this precious saint had died. I began wrestling about whether I should stay at the retreat (I also had another message to preach the following night) or drive back home to minister to the woman's faithful son. I soon felt that the Lord wanted me to go back and shepherd my flock. First Peter 5:2 says, *"Shepherd the flock of God among you, exercising oversight not under compulsion, but voluntarily, according to the will of God; and not for sordid gain, but with eagerness."* It was not only my duty to go back to Paradise to minister to this grieving son but it was a joy and delight to do so.

Before this man and I had a chance to pray this morning, he asked a special request. The funeral home had lost some records showing that his mother had prepaid for her funeral, and he was going to have to talk to them about it. On top of that, the funeral home charged extra for a Sunday funeral (which he is having due a scheduling conflict with one of the participants). I could tell he was not happy about all of this, and so I prayed Proverbs 21:1 for him and that the Lord would show him favor with the funeral directors.

He called me as I was driving back to the retreat cabin to tell me that God answers prayers. It turned out that son of the funeral home owner was playing baseball on Saturday, and he really wanted to make it to that game. Because a Saturday funeral would be out of the question, the funeral director offered and agreed to pay the extra expenses for a Sunday funeral.

Why are we surprised when God comes through? Shouldn't it be the other way around—shouldn't you and I be perplexed and baffled when our prayers go unanswered? It is time to quit making excuses and to start praying in such a way that we see much accomplished.

I have been nibbling on this very thought for the past four days. What can God really do when He unleashes His power? More specifically, I have asked this question in light of the implications on our church in Paradise. I keep feeling this burden down deep to ask and believe for our church to double in attendance over the next nine months. This kind of attendance would take us into uncharted waters, and it would take me into uncharted waters in my ministry as well. Is that a hard thing for God? Isn't it the will of God to reach more people? Would God get the glory for it? Absolutely!

Accomplishing much or *availing much* has several different meaning in the original languages. Prayers that accomplish much are prayers that *see large results, abundant results, and great results.* So does that define the answers to our prayers? Typically, our results are few and far between, miniscule and infinitesimal. But God gets great glory out of great praying that accomplishes *much*! In order for this happen, however, several things must take place.

First, we must be *pure* before the Lord. Scriptures like 1 John 1:9 are a great help at this point: *"If we confess our sins, He is faithful and righteous to forgive us our sins and to cleanse us from all unrighteousness."* We must maintain a pure heart before the Lord, but even in working hard to do that, we are still not worthy to pray. We are made righteous only one way: *"He made Him who knew no sin to be sin on our behalf, that we might become the righteousness of God in Him"* (2 Cor. 5:21). Jesus makes us righteous. We need to accept and claim that fact if we are to pray in such a way that God answers abundantly and largely.

Next, our petitions need to be *fervent.* They must be passionately offered with zeal—no half-hearted wishing. They must be effective, and in order to be so there must be faith and determination to be heard and to seize the answer. There is so little determination mixed with bold belief for the Lord to answer much of our praying. We say all the right words, but the truth is, we do not believe much of what we are saying. God knows whether we believe or don't believe. God sees our hearts and knows whether our petitions are forged in the fires of faith or crafted in the caverns of doubt and dismay.

When we pray fervently in faith, God releases power to show up in our situations in ways that boggle the mind and stagger the knees. Our prayers truly become effective. Miracles follow and testimonies flow unceasingly. What is fervent praying? It is *active* and *efficient* praying. It is prayer that demonstrates the power of God; therefore it is prayer that secures the answer desired and displays the enduring faithfulness of the Lord in all situations and during all seasons of life. Fervent praying is also *consistent* praying. Whether God is allowing His streams of abundance to flow our way or we are walking through the valley of the shadow of death, our prayers must remain constant.

I have been reading a biography of a mighty man of prayer named Reese Howells. During a season of praying the Lord required Howells to pray for a certain lost man who was a drunk. Howells was not to witness to the man or to tell anyone he was praying for his salvation but to take his petitions to the Lord alone. Soon the Lord also required him to believe for the salvation of one the hardest women in the whole community. Howells prayed for these two for months and even came to a point where the Lord told him not to pray any longer, that any additional prayers would be a sign of doubt. He was to be *convinced* that both would be saved. Eventually, both of those people came to Jesus, demonstrating once again that fervent and effectual praying can accomplish much. The word *much* means "abundant, large, many, numerous, and great." Does that definition characterize your prayer life or mine?

Another one of God's prayer warriors demonstrated the power of fervent and effectual prayer in his life. His name was John Hyde (better known as Praying Hyde), and he served as a missionary to India. During a convention in 1908, Hyde took the courageous step of asking the Lord for one soul to be saved each day of that year. He prayed and witnessed unceasingly during that year, and near the start of the same convention a year later in 1909, Hyde checked his records and found that over 400 souls had been won to Christ that year, more than he had asked for.

During the 1909 convention, God put a burden on Hyde to believe for *two* souls to be saved each day the following year. Again Hyde prayed fervently and witnessed with tireless zeal. By the start of the 1910 convention, a total of 800 souls had been saved under Hyde's ministry. *That* is prayer that accomplishes much.

God's next challenge to Hyde was to believe for *four* souls to be saved each day of that year. The burden was great, but Hyde's faith and praying were greater. Read what Basil Miller records of Hyde during this period in his book, *Praying Hyde*:

> And when Hyde returned to the field, he lost sight of all else save those four souls each day. He once told a friend that if on any day four souls were not brought into the fold, at night there would be such

a weight on his heart that it was positively painful, and he could not eat or sleep.[7]

Hyde demonstrated year after year what James said in our Scripture for this chapter—the fervent and effectual prayers of a righteous man or woman can accomplish amazing things. The trouble is, few people really want to be put in a position like Howells or Hyde to be tried in their faith in such a public way. It is much safer and more comfortable to live by sight and not faith; yet this is the very cutting edge of prayer. It was on the anvil of these kinds of tests that faith has been tried and proven true over and over again. So it must be with you and me.

Let me conclude this chapter with a personal story about prayer that accomplished much. I will never forget early one morning about seven years ago as I was tossing and turning, not able to sleep, at around 2:30 when suddenly the silence of our dark bedroom was broken by Brenda's meek voice: "Are you asleep?"

I told her that I could not sleep, and she informed me that sleep was escaping her too that night. What was keeping us from being able to sleep? We both were feeling that the Lord was calling her to leave a fifteen-year career with J C Penney—a job at which she had been highly sucessful and was making over $50,000 a year—to stay at home and raise our growing family of boys. With me constantly on the road and an increase in the number of nights she was required to work each week, Brenda had come to realize that God had not given us children for daycare workers or babysitters to raise. So we made the decision that she would stay home

---

7 Basil Miller, *Praying Hyde* (Greenville: Ambassador, 2000), p. 103.

with them, even though I didn't have a concrete means of supporting us other than what the Lord prompted people to give to No Compromise. We were about to take a giant leap of faith and trust the Lord to help us make it only on my salary from No Compromise Ministries, which was less than $24,000 a year at the time.

People told us we were foolish. Many so-called "friends" said we would fail, while others were worried about us. Yet, as we have done countless times before and since, when we feel we have heard from God, we leap. It was incredibly difficult, and we have gone through some very lean times in the nine years since that decision. We have been tested, and at times we have both thought it was foolish for her to have abandoned her career; yet nine years later, we are still making it. We eat well, and we have more than we need. We are closer to being completely out of debt than we have ever been. It has never been easy, but we know the Lord honors our prayers for provision. For nine years the skeptics have been unable to do anything but hang their heads in amazement as God has done miracle after miracle to meet our needs. It has been a difficult but adventuresome journey, and one in which I can say the Lord has honored His Word.

Today I serve at a wonderful church as pastor and make a lot more than $24,000 a year. Brenda still stays home, or I should say she is a homemaker (but does the equivalent of a full-time job volunteering at the school and serving at the church). My family is strong, and we are united, and we continue to believe the Lord to do a miracle to *give* us a house (with deed in hand, debt-free). Why, this is just another one of those public tests the Lord has put before us. We still stand on the promise that fervent and effectual prayer can accomplish much—*very much*! We started praying for this house before we ever moved to Paradise. Three years later we continue to wait and pray, but we cling to the word the Lord spoke to me in this very prayer cabin over a year ago: "Matt, I desire to give you a house in Paradise. Trust Me for it and behold My faithfulness once again."

I know most who read this will doubt the validity of what I sensed the Lord saying that morning in an empty prayer retreat. I know people think I am off my rocker and that I am presuming upon God. I have heard all of this before, yet still I believe. Brenda and I have searched all over Paradise and looked at many houses. We have clung to the promise when it all looked hopeless. We have also been very specific in asking for a house, as I told you about in chapter 5. We continue to wait for the house He has for us; it's just a matter of time and waiting for Him to move. You will be able to drive to Paradise and visit us in a miracle house we are trusting the Lord for, in His timing. That will demonstrate prayer that accomplishes much.

CHAPTER 12

Nothing is Impossible

"With people this is impossible, but with God all things are possible" (Matt. 19:26).

"For nothing will be impossible with God" (Luke 1:37).

"Ah Lord GOD! Behold, You have made the heavens and the earth by Your great power and by Your outstretched arm! Nothing is too difficult for You" (Jer. 32:17).

Life is filled with impossibilities. Millions live in absolute poverty, believing it is impossible for them to ever own their own home or live in relative financial security. Thousands upon thousands of husbands and wives live together in marriages that have lost their romantic fizzle. These couples cohabit for numerous reasons but do not enjoy each other's company and have lost their passion for each another. Though they may remain married, they have lost all hope of really falling head over heels in love again as they did when they were first dating or on the day they exchanged their wedding vows.

How many are plagued and tormented by dreams that have never been fulfilled? These souls live with the despair of chasing after a dream that resembles a carrot dangling in front of them that they never get to taste or enjoy. In frustration many have given up and thrown in the towel on these dreams. The death of a vision never comes easy, and believe me, I know firsthand. Watching your dreams fade into the murky shadows of impossibility is a difficult thing to endure.

Still others live with daily chronic pain that aggravates and exaggerates every other trial in life. Sleep does not come easily, leading to increased fatigue. The famous Vince Lombardi, former football coach of the Green Bay Packers, said, "Fatigue makes cowards of us all."[8] Fatigue can often lead into bouts of depression. Millions fight this battle, and as one woman I recently heard testified, "I cope with life thanks to prayer and Prozac."

Countless numbers live under the cloak of darkness and despair, unable to find hope for living, unable to enjoy life, feeling trapped, just trying to survive. There are those who think that seeing this cloak of darkness ever lift is impossible.

Every day somebody is diagnosed with some illness or disease that seems impossible to cure despite expensive medical treatments, like cancer, heart disease, MS, Lou Gehrig's disease—and the list goes on. These diseases often drag the patients down a slippery slope of hopelessness offering no way of escape. Healing seems impossible.

Yes, on the surface each of these situations seems *impossible*. Yet in each of these situations possibilities abound if God steps in to flex His mighty muscle to move each mountain. If God wills to whisk away these same impossibilities, we will come to know firsthand what countless people throughout the ages have come to learn—*nothing is impossible with God!*

---

[8] www.brainquote.com.quotes/authors/v/vince_lombardi.html

That is the exact message the young virgin Mary learned when she was given the precious promise of giving birth to the Savior of the Word. The angel Gabriel gave her words that would forever change her life: "*For nothing will be impossible with God*" (Luke 1:37). That message found fertile soil in the heart of this young woman, though being impregnated by the Holy Spirit while remaining a virgin must have seemed outlandish. Mary *did* believe nothing was impossible with the Lord, and she gave her response in Luke 1:38: "*Behold, the bondslave of the Lord; may it be done to me according to your word.*"

God is looking for bondslaves who refuse to be duped and deceived by seemingly impossible circumstances, those who understand that nothing is impossible with God. The Lord is looking for people of all ages who believe that nothing is impossible with God. Nothing! Just today I had a sixteen-year-old young man come into my office to tell me that God is calling him to give his life to be a full-time missionary. Wow! He doesn't see the task the Lord has called him to as impossible; he believes God has not only *called* him but will *equip* him to go into the nations to make the name of Jesus famous despite cultural and language barriers.

Mary used the word *bondslave* to describe her status before God, and her word choice was no accident. In the biblical culture bondslaves had no rights; the purpose of their existence was to please their masters. This is not a popular picture of discipleship in this modern age. What people don't understand, however, is that as a bondslave you get to be on a mission, not just *for* God but *with* God. What is more exciting than to watch God do the impossible and to watch Him do it through *you*?

154

Nothing is impossible when God works through surren-dered bondslaves. Nothing is impossible for God to fix, solve, restore, heal, provide, or forgive. That means that any marriage can be restored, despite years of neglect and abuse. I know a couple whose marriage hit rock bottom. The hus-band was an insensitive workaholic, and the wife was an emotional wreck. They were close to divorce when the hus-band read one long neglected verse: *" 'For I hate divorce,' says the LORD, the God of Israel, 'and him who covers his garment with wrong,' says the LORD of hosts. 'So take heed to your spirit, that you do not deal treacherously'"* (Mal. 2:16).

This couple took God at His word when they read that He hates divorce, and they eliminated that option from their list of choices. It took some work and a lot of prayer, but the impossible marriage was restored, and today those two people act like a couple of newlyweds most of the time, often slipping off for romantic getaways. They asked God to do the impossible by restoring their marriage, and God did just that; their testimony is that God can save *any* marriage when given the chance.

As you read this, I am confident that you have your own impossible situation and you will eventually find yourself on one side of this promise or the other. You will either rise up in faith, or you will shrink in doubt. You can choose to believe that God is a God who keeps His Word and is faithful to ten thousand generations. You can choose to trust that God delights to answer the desperate, faith-filled prayers of those facing impossible circumstances. You will choose this course, or you will live in doubt and remain a skeptic—it is a choice you will have to make.

God's Word is a rock-solid foundation on which you can build your life and the hopes and dreams of your family and even future generations. But multitudes build their lives and their families' futures on the sinking sands of their own strength and the wisdom of this world. The former will leave you with God's bountiful blessings, and the latter will leave you with a life in disarray (Matt. 7:24-27).

Making a statement like "nothing is impossible with God" is huge! The implications are as broad as the ocean and as deep as the seas. Immediately the question surfaces: Can this promise from the Lord of Hosts be taken literally? Does God really mean this? Is Luke 1:37 the only place in Scripture where such a statement is made?

Abraham and Sarah learned that nothing was impossible with God when they were promised a son, even though decades passed before the fulfillment of this promise, leaving them both past the typical child-bearing stage. When they were both well advanced in years, the promise of a son was again given with a definite and measurable time frame for its fulfillment. An angel of the Lord spoke to Abraham, saying, *"I will surely return to you at this time next year; and behold, Sarah your wife will have a son."* Sarah heard all of this and laughed in doubt, and the angel responded swiftly, saying, *"Is anything too difficult for the LORD? At the appointed time I will return to you, at this time next year, and Sarah will have a son"* (Gen. 18:10,14).

And that is exactly what happened! God blessed Abraham and Sarah with Isaac, a true miracle child. God had performed an impossible miracle, as it is also recorded in Romans 4:18-21. Even the physical laws of nature can be bent to accomplish the sovereign choices of our God, again proving that nothing is impossible with His intervention.

The prophet Jeremiah's confession of faith says, *"Ah Lord GOD! Behold, You have made the heavens and the earth by Your great power and by Your outstretched arm! Nothing is too difficult for You"* (Jer. 32:17). Saying that nothing is too difficult for God is just like saying that nothing is impossible. Another declaration is made in this same chapter, but this time by the Lord Himself: *"Behold, I am the LORD, the God of all flesh; is anything too difficult for Me?"* (Jer. 32:27). The answer to this question is most assuredly *no*. No, there is not anything that is too difficult for our God to manage.

Jesus continued this same line of thought on multiple occasions. In Matthew 19:26 He said, *"With people this is impossible, but with God all things are possible."* Jesus is stating the same truth found in Luke 1:37 in another way. Luke 18:27 reiterates the same point by saying, *"The things that are impossible with people are possible with God."*

My question is—why do we not live like we really believe this? We are far too quick to explain away this truth and make excuses as to why we cannot apply the principle to our circumstances.

During our eighteen-month extreme faith makeover, we tried to diligently obey the Lord's command to not ask anyone for money. We took our needs to the Lord and trusted Him to meet them, whatever they were. It was a very trying time. Over and over again we would be stretched to the limit. Just when we had lost all hope, God would do another miracle and remind us that nothing is ever impossible for Him.

I recall one particular Sunday when we really needed a financial miracle. I had just finished teaching a Bible study to a small handful of people in our living room. We never took up an offering during our times of worship and study of the Word; we placed a small basket on the bar overlooking our kitchen and trusted God to prompt people to give. We *never*

157

made mention of that basket on any Sunday, but after people left for their homes, we would often gather around that basket to see how the Lord had provided for another week (or on some occasions, for another day).

That particular Sunday we were desperate. We needed money to buy groceries and were really counting on our people to give. Our cupboard was nearly bare, and we did not have any money to buy even the bare necessities, like milk, bread, or eggs. We committed the matter to the Lord and rested, assured that He would provide as He had done countless times before. After teaching a message from the book of Luke in our primitive little service, I walked outside onto our driveway to visit with the people before they left. Brenda went back inside before I did, but when I walked through the front door, her expression said it all—the basket was empty.

I couldn't believe that no one had given even a dollar that morning. Brenda was dejected, I was dejected, and my initial response was doubt and anger at God and anger at those who made up our little house church but who seemingly did not understand the financial pressure we were under and who had ignored our great need.

We rummaged up something for lunch, and I retired to our bedroom to watch a ballgame and take a nap, hoping to forget about the whole matter. We determined once again to leave it in God's hands.

Later that afternoon our doorbell rang. One of our most faithful couples, Mark and Sandy, were standing in the doorway. They were out running an errand and remembered they had forgotten to tithe that morning. They handed us a folded check, which we later discovered was for over $350. God had reminded them about their tithe, and instead of waiting until the next week to give like many would have done, they made a special trip to our house to give to the Lord, unknowingly becoming the conduit for our miraculous answer to prayer. Thanks to that check, we were able to buy groceries and gas and take care of other necessities the following week. What looked impossible at one point became more than possible only a few hours later; that is how it is with God. If we could things see from His perspective all the time we would truly be convinced that nothing is impossible with God.

We wrote Mark and Sandy a letter to testify how the Lord had used them to answer our prayers that week, and we were never again in that situation after that. In fact, I often saw them looking through our cabinets on Sunday mornings to make sure we had enough food.

Brenda and the boys and I celebrated God's faithfulness that Sunday afternoon. We testified to the boys that God had done another miracle and had once again proved that nothing was impossible with Him.

Perhaps no other personal story I could tell about lessons learned during that eighteen-month period can illustrate that nothing is impossible with God better than the one I am about to relate. Our family was driving down the main thoroughfare in Lufkin one day when suddenly the whole van began to jerk, lurch back and forth, and make a horrible noise. I quickly turned into the first parking lot I could find, which happened to be a Chinese restaurant, and we coasted to a stop. No matter what gear I put it in, the van remained motionless. The transmission had gone out. My Jeep had already broken down on my way home from a preaching trip to San Angelo, so that van was our only means of transportation.

I called a friend to pick us up and then, completely on faith, called a transmission repair shop to tow the van in to be fixed. We did not have extra money to pay for *any* car repairs, much less to have a new transmission installed. We were now without transportation, and I trusted that God would provide in some way. I reckoned that God knew we were in great need once again, the van was our only means of transportation, and therefore God would supply all the money needed to repair the van.

The news from the repair shop was not good, however, and the total cost of the necessary repairs was around $1,800. We did not have the money, but I was confident that God would meet the need before the van was running again.

About a week later the repair shop called, informing me that the van was ready to be picked up. It was a Friday evening, but we had not yet received any miracle. I thought to myself that God would meet the need by the following Monday, since we couldn't pick up the van over the weekend anyway. In the meantime we borrowed a vehicle from friends, a 1993 Suburban with 290,000 miles on it. But then Monday came and went...with no miracle.

We prayed and prayed. Tuesday passed, and then Wednesday, Thursday, Friday, and so on. *No miracle.* Two weeks went by. Finally, in total humiliation I had to call the owner of the shop to tell him about our situation. I promised that we would pay the bill in full when we got the money and would not pick the van up until then. The owner was very kind, but I knew he needed the money to provide for his own family.

Three weeks passed. A very limited number of friends knew about our plight: the ones who picked us up the day of trial and the ones who let us borrow their Suburban.

At the end of the fourth week, the repair shop called late on a Friday afternoon while I was coaching Tucker's t-ball team. The owner told me to pick the van up—because the bill had been *paid in full*. My knees nearly buckled when I heard those words! Once again God had heard and responded to our frantic prayers and had done the impossible. The repair shop owner never did tell me who paid for the repairs, and the two families who knew about the situation both insisted they had nothing to do with it.

I brought the van home and gave the keys to Brenda, and later she found an envelope in the van with a $100 bill inside and a short note reminding us of the faithfulness of God.

Wanting to celebrate, we called our good friends Jeff and Melissa to meet us for lunch at the same Chinese restaurant where the van had broken down. We used the $100 to buy lunch for both of our families and to celebrate God's faithfulness. Getting the van out of the shop had seemed impossible, but God showed that it was really no big deal. This is another one of the stories I have been able to recount in pulpits all over the state of Texas in order to give God glory. To this day I have no idea who paid for the repairs on that van, but I know that whoever did it did so because the Lord prompted them to.

How do you explain a miracle like that? We didn't go around advertising our need to people everywhere; in fact, most people didn't know about the situation until after it was over. However *you* choose to explain it, I choose to believe that God took an impossible situation—I did not have $1,800—and *made* it possible. He provided all the money needed to repair the van and made provision for a vehicle for us to drive in the interim. His power is *never* exhausted. His strength *never* fails or weakens regardless of the size of the burden.

No circumstance is beyond His control. No mountain is immovable. No situation is beyond His ability to solve. No thing, no trial, no problem, no need, no burden—*nothing*—is beyond His control. He has proven this over and over again through the pages of history and in the lives of countless saints.

Look at Lazarus; he had a major problem—he was dead. Not even this situation, however, was impossible for Jesus to deal with.

> *Jesus said to her, "Did I not say to you that if you believe, you will see the glory of God?" So they removed the stone. Then Jesus raised His eyes, and said, "Father, I thank You that You have heard Me. I knew that You always hear Me; but because of the people standing around I said it, so that they may believe that You sent Me." When He had said these things, He cried out with a loud voice, "Lazarus, come forth." The man who had died came forth, bound hand and foot with wrappings, and his face was wrapped around with a cloth. Jesus said to them, "Unbind him, and let him go"* (John 11:40-44).

Dead men do not normally awake from the dead; nor do they walk out of their graves, but death is not impossible for Jesus to overcome. In fact, He *defeated* death only a few chapters later in the Gospel of John. If *death* is not an impossible situation for Jesus, what is left?

This same Jesus raised the widow's son (Luke 7:11-17) and Jairus' daughter (Mark 5:21-42). If even death cannot oppose our God and falls in defeat before Him, what else can stand in His way? *Nothing*! Not death, disease, divorce, abuse, neglect, racism, poverty, lostness, immorality—nothing is beyond His ability.

Are you so arrogant as you read this chapter as to have exalted yourself and your problems to a place of prominence where God cannot help you? Will you be the first person who has lived from Adam to today who will be able to stand up and say, "My problem proved to be too difficult for God to handle"? Are your mountains so mammoth that Jehovah's knees buckle under their weight and He fails to stand up under the pressure of your burdens? No, and a thousand times no!

If nothing is impossible, that means that now and forevermore this promise stands like the rock of Gibraltar—our God never fails! *Ever*! When wisdom is needed during times of confusion, His wisdom is made available (Jas. 1:5). When provision is the need of the hour, He supplies, never exhausting the treasures of His storehouse (Phil. 4:19). When strength is needed to carry on during times of trial, His strength is readily available (Isa. 41:10).

Let me conclude this chapter with an impossible miracle story. Over the Thanksgiving weekend, a young man in our church named Scott was hanging Christmas lights on the roof of his house. As he reached out to his side to attach some lights to a section of his roof, his ladder slipped, causing him to crash to the ground from about fourteen feet in the air. All of his weight landed on one leg and ankle, shattering bones in dozens of pieces (so many that the doctors quit counting). Paramedics came to his rescue, and he was transported by LifeFlight to a hospital in Fort Worth, where I drove to meet him and his family.

The prognosis for Scott's injury was not very good; he was looking at several tricky operations with no guarantees of ever being able to walk or be active again. At one point, the doctors discovered that he actually had a piece of bone missing. Our church began praying for a miracle; we asked God to help the surgeons so that Scott would not have to have a bone graft to fill in the hole left by the missing bone. Several surgeries ensued.

Scott had a lengthy stay in the hospital, and things did not get easier when he was released to go home just before Christmas. He had to lie in bed flat on his back with his leg elevated for twenty-three hours out of every twenty-four-hour period. It was a grueling recovering process. Many doubted that Scott would ever walk again, but I kept asking God for a miracle. My prayer was not only that he would walk again but also that he would be able to return to at least some of his former activities as a well-loved coach, principal, and father.

I will never forget the day in late January when Scott came back to church for the first time, in a wheelchair with his leg elevated in front of him. He wept through most of the service, as did many of those around him. He went back to work as junior high principal in the early spring, coached my son Tanner's baseball team, and started to play golf again. Yesterday he told me he had played a round of golf just the other day. As far as his injury, X-rays showed new bone growth in place of the missing piece, even though no graft had been done. Nothing short of a miracle.

Today Scott walks with hardly any limp at all. He coached his son's little league basketball and baseball teams this past year, achieved a postgraduate degree, is now the high school principal, and he even joined the choir at church. I have even seen him run briefly on this ankle when many doubted he would ever walk again, much less run.

Don't tell this man or his family that anything is impossible with God—he is living a miracle every single day. My prayer now is that he will able to continue the very active lifestyle he enjoyed before that fall.

There will be many times in our lives when we face impossible situations. The question is, what will we believe about God in those moments? Brenda and I have some friends back in East Texas who have traveled this road many times. When we lived in East Texas they were trying to have a second child and had great difficulty conceiving. They went to several different doctors for second and third opinions but left those consultations just as confused as they were before they went. At times they were told that their chances of conceiving were less than 10 percent. During this time, I went off to my little prayer cabin and was praying for them. I became convinced that it was the Lord's will to bless them with a child to join the handsome little boy they already had. Sure enough, several months later they became pregnant and were ecstatic.

But joy turned to heartache when tests showed that the little baby girl had a chromosome disorder, and doctors expected that she would not live long enough to see her first birthday. I refused to believe this diagnosis, and prayers were offered up by myself and by others by the hundreds.

On the day that the little girl was born and everyone went to the hospital to visit, I stayed behind in my home office to pray. I did not entertain one doubt about the Lord healing that precious baby and showing everyone His power. My faith was severely tested, however, when less than two months later Brenda and I stood in the back of an overcrowded funeral home at that little girl's funeral. I did not understand it—I had felt so confident that it was the Lord's will to give that couple another child.

Time went by, and the wife started a ministry in her church for others who had experienced the loss of an infant, which God continues to use to this day. The grief, however, was still there. She became pregnant again soon after and lost that baby to a miscarriage, a tragedy that was repeated numerous times. It was a heart-wrenching journey for this couple, but Brenda and I continued to believe that it was God's will to bless them with a second child.

A little less than a year ago, they became pregnant again. Everyone held their breath through each phase of the pregnancy, but the baby appeared to be healthy. We were awakened early one morning by a phone call—the baby had arrived, and everything was fine! We hurriedly got ready, loaded up the boys, and drove over four hours to Nacogdoches, Texas, to the same hospital where Taylor, Tanner, and Tucker had been born. What an absolute joy to see that beautiful miracle baby and the radiant faces of our friends and their son, who was so proud to be a big brother. We celebrated God's victory over that seemingly impossible situation.

I exhort you to take your impossible situation and lay it before the Lord, who can make all things possible. Give it to God, and then walk away, leaving your impossible situation with Him. Wait and watch what happens. You may have to wait longer than you would like, but if you wait long enough you too will discover firsthand that nothing is impossible with God. You will then share that testimony over and over again with broken people who need to hear it, inspiring hope and confidence in their walk with God. Then they too will discover what so many others before have learned: *Nothing is impossible with God!*

CHAPTER 13

Praying with Confidence

This is the confidence which we have before Him, that, if we ask anything according to His will, He hears us. And if we know that He hears us in whatever we ask, we know that we have the requests which we have asked from Him (1 John 5:14-15).

Don't you wish you could pray in such a way that you know for certain you will get what you asked for? Is it possible to grow in your prayer life until you have such great confidence in God that doubt is not able to find a lodging place in your heart or mind? My friends, it *is* possible to pray with simple faith and to have unwavering confidence that you will receive what you have asked for.

George Mueller, the great prayer warrior, founded and operated orphanages completely on faith, without ever asking anyone for money to help support the thousands of orphans. He was about to board an ocean liner with his wife for an extended preaching trip when he was informed that a special-order chair for his wife had not yet arrived. Mrs. Mueller suffered severely from seasickness, and the special chair was designed to help in this matter. An official from the ship recommended that arrangements for another chair be made immediately. But Mueller refused to budge. He had prayed over this chair and felt confident that God would bring it in time, though the ship was scheduled to depart very soon. The ship's official did not share Mueller's faith and expressed his sentiments. When the ship was only minutes from launching out into the deep, the official once again urged the Muellers to secure another chair before it was too late. Again Mueller stood in confident faith that God would supply the very chair they had prayed for and ordered in advance.

Just before the ship was about to depart, a man on shore began waving and yelling frantically. He was delivering the very chair the Muellers had been trusting God to provide. And guess who had to take delivery of the chair? Yes, you guessed it. The very official who had doubted God would provide it at all.

How could George Mueller remain so confident in such a distressing situation in the face of repeated verbal doubts expressed by the ship's official? Wouldn't it have made more sense to just secure another chair? Mueller was courageously confident that the chair would arrive on time, just like he had been day in and day out that the Lord would supply the food and clothing needed to take care of all of those orphans. He had seen God come through thousands of times. Having beheld God's faithfulness for decades made it that much easier to trust Him for a simple chair to aid his wife on the sea voyage.

Does the modern-day Church pray with this kind of confidence? There are innumerable books written on the subject of prayer. I have many in my library at the church and have read most of them. These days there are prayer retreats, conferences, seminars, and even studies on prayer, but despite all of this, confident praying is rare, even among faithful Christians. The thing is, it is one thing to study about prayer and quite another to actually pray!

Though most of today's believers would be quick to say they believe in the power of prayer, few know real confidence in their prayers. God does not get the kind of glory He deserves from much of our praying, because we pray without confidence that He will answer.

One thing that gave George Mueller great confidence in God's ability to answer prayer was reading through his Bible, 200 times throughout his lifetime. His faith and confidence were enlarged with every subsequent reading, helping him to treasure the precious promises of God. If men and women today could gain the kind of confidence in praying that Mueller had, the results would be just as dramatic as the things he witnessed.

The word *confidence* in 1 John 5:14 literally means "outspokenness, frankness, bluntness, and publicity." That is what Mueller did with the ship's official—he *publicized* what he was believing God to do. He spoke about his confident expectation openly, frankly, and publicly. Far too many of us claim to believe in prayer but harbor lingering doubt in the deep caverns of our souls. So how many books and conferences does it take to shore up the walls of confidence in the lives of present-day disciples? It is my prayer that this book will help do that. I hope that as you read about God's amazing work in the Edwards household you will be encouraged and inspired to pray with greater confidence.

You see, confident praying is *crucial* to the advancement of God's kingdom. You can define this kingdom as "the rule and reign of God." Confident intercession is also crucial in the role of missions around the globe. It is crucial for your future and that of your family. So how do you go about increasing the confidence factor in your petitions?

I believe that this is something you *can* learn and grow in. But if you desire to grow in this area, you are going to have to be willing to *exercise* your faith. Faith is like a muscle and has the ability to grow in strength and stamina when exposed to pressure. The only way to gain this strength and stamina is to willingly submit yourself to situations where you have to depend on God.

It's no wonder we have such little and weak faith—we are rarely put in situations where we have to depend on God. We depend on our health, our wisdom, our connections, our families and friends, but only in the most drastic situations do most of us have to depend on God. During these times of testing, we are forced to see God come through as we plead for help, or else we fall on our faces.

Our eighteen-month test of faith was not about us. It was about God demonstrating to us first and to those all around us that a person can really take God at His word and live a life fully reliant on Him to meet every need. I have learned through personal experience that our confidence increases each time we behold God's faithfulness. The confident prayers may start small and the corresponding results may seem small and insignificant, but over time as confidence grows, so will the prayers. You will begin believing God for things that seem audacious to doubters, like that ship's official. You will keep trusting and asking and never mind the doubters.

I was not saved until I was seventeen years old. Though I grew a lot as a teenager in the Denman Avenue Baptist Church youth group in Lufkin, I do not recall growing much in my prayer life. Looking back over that period of my life, I cannot recall one specific answer to prayer. I can only recall one incident when I really had to depend on God. My mother was very sick and needed quadruple bypass heart surgery. At the time I was scared out of my mind, but my youth minister exhorted me to trust God to take care of her. Other than that, I did not see much tangible evidence of God working through prayer. My prayer life was weak because I had weak faith. But the year I enrolled as a freshman at Howard Payne University, I was really introduced to the power of prayer, as I mentioned earlier. It was also there that I was put into the first situation where I *had* to depend on God.

I went to Howard Payne on a partial football scholarship, which means that my scholarship did not cover the full cost of room, board, and tuition. My mother and I had to come up with the remainder of the money by the end of the semester or I would not be allowed to take my final exams, meaning I would get incompletes in all my classes. My mother could not help me, however, because at the time she was trying to recover from surgery.

Early one morning before classes, I sat in a prayer huddle and shared my financial burden, asking the guys to pray with me. That small prayer meeting led by upperclassman Byron Schueller made a lasting impact on my life. Byron shared devotional thoughts from Matthew 6:27-33 that day, and through those verses God gave me confidence in Him for the first time in my life. We lifted up the need in prayer, and I left it with God, trusting Him to handle it. I had confidence that He would come through. I did not fret or worry but kept asking Him to work it out—and amazingly, He did. I don't know how He did it, but I do know that if God had not provided that money, there was no backup plan. My football practice schedule on top of my class schedule left me no time to find a part-time job. God *had* to come through, or I was sunk. I asked, and He intervened and provided every penny I needed.

The next several years were a continuation this stretching of my faith, as God provided a car for me through the Munden family of Rochelle Baptist Church, called me to go to seminary and went before me to prepare the way with a job and housing, and later opened another door for me to serve the Spring Creek Baptist Church in Weatherford as youth minister. Brenda and I were married one month after me taking that position, and we moved to Weatherford, where our joint journey in faith began that would take us over high mountains and through some of the darkest valleys either of us had ever known.

As you can see from the pilgrimage I have been sharing with you, God has been continually leading me and stretching me, forging faith in the midst of trials and seemingly impossible situations. Yet with each miracle, I have believed God more and learned more about the power of prayer.

While at seminary I spent countless hours in the library, not studying for classes or writing papers but reading about prayer. I loved to find out about God's warriors from the past, educate myself about their lives and exploits for God, and read what they wrote on the subject of prayer and faith. As I absorbed the faith and confidence of those mighty men of God, my confidence continued to grow.

Through it all, I have learned over the past twenty years that it is right and necessary to pray with confidence. God *expects* it. That is why I was willing to obey God when He told me not to get a secular job after the collapse of

CentrePointe Community Church and not to ask anyone for money but to trust Him to meet our every need. This was the culmination of a decade of faith-building and training. Now, I did not know how long that season was going to last when I took those first steps of obedience, but I wouldn't trade the miracles I was able to witness during the year and half to follow. Each of those miracles is like a signpost along the path Brenda and I have taken toward true confidence in God.

Today as I write this I sit in a small apartment in Abilene, Texas, where I will be preaching to a group of teenagers this week. Looking back, I can see how all of this was preparation for bringing me to First Baptist Church of Paradise as pastor. I knew all along that God would put me in a situation to serve Him that would require great faith. Great faith is needed to solve the space problems we are now experiencing at the church. Our parking lot is now full, and many Sundays we have people parking up and down the main street on each side. A few families have to park at a café about a quarter of mile away and walk to church each Sunday. Our Sunday school classes are full, and we need to add additional classes, but we do not have empty classrooms available, and I literally mean that we do not have *one single empty classroom* on any given Sunday morning. We actually have one class meeting near the church in the home of the teacher. We have already added a second Sunday morning worship service, and the biggest problem of all is that we are completely landlocked—we don't have a square foot to expand anywhere. As I think about all of these issues, I know for certain that all of my faith trials have been preparation for such a time as this. I can face these problems with confidence in God.

In fact, in recent days the Lord has called us to partner with some churches in the province of Saskatchewan in Canada. I received an e-mail today asking our church to help not just one church but possibly four or five in that area. This is something that is much bigger than the walls of our church, but after decades of learning to trust God, I am eager to leap into this adventure and to lead our church in a jump in faith and trust God to do what we cannot do ourselves.

I am writing this book in complete confidence that God will make a way to have it published. Right now no doors are open, but my trust is that God will either provide the money to publish it through No Compromise Ministries or will open a door through a publishing company. Why would anyone want to publish a book from an unknown author with a string of ministry failures in his wake? The answer is, they wouldn't, but *God* would. I absolutely believe that God has called me to write, but I also believe that He inspired and has given birth to this book. I believed by faith that while this book is still in manuscript form the Lord would get it into the hands of people like you who will grow and be encouraged in their prayer lives. Therefore, I continue pecking away on this keyboard to take this book from the frail form of ideas to the concrete reality of the printed page.

There are no shortcuts on the road to developing fervent faith and passionate prayer. There will be countless hours spent in the shadows of solitude locked away with God, wrestling with Him over burdens and needs. At times, these hours isolate us from family and friends and can produce loneliness. Yet I know that it is in these dark and hidden places that men and women of prayer are shaped. Trials fall at the feet of Mighty God as prayers flow without ceasing.

There will always be something to trust God for; therefore our confidence in God must be ever growing, and that means being tested again and again. That means the Lord will continually lead and nudge us into impossible situations like Moses at the Red Sea, Daniel in the lions' den, Elijah on Mount Carmel, David facing Goliath, or Gideon fighting with only 300 men.

I remember a few years ago bringing a huge trial before Him and admitting that I could not overcome the trial without the divine intervention of Jehovah. It dawned on me then that if I really wanted to be a man devoted to prayer, I would always be facing trials and always be put in a position where prayer would be my only means of escape. I then asked the Lord to keep testing my faith in order to make it strong, knowing that this prayer could have lifelong implications.

Don't be discouraged by the fact that your faith must be tested in order to grow your confidence in the Lord. Think of all the fresh testimonies you will have of God's enduring faithfulness. You will be an eyewitness to miracles, and you will also have the opportunity to pass the torch of faith to those the Lord has gathered around you, like children, grandchildren, and friends.

At the beginning of this book I related the story of how God birthed this book in my heart. Getting it published was a whole different story. For years I prayed and prayed for God to open a door to get this book into print. All doors remained firmly shut. Prayers for financial provision went unanswered, or at least I thought they were unanswered.

After several years I was praying one Sunday morning in my office before the start of our early service when I sensed the Lord leading me to do three things. I sensed Him leading me to ask our church to pray with me and believe with me for money to buy a parsonage for a staff member we wanted to call to our church. I sensed Him leading me to ask the congregation to pray and believe with me for a vehicle for a needy family in our community whom had never set foot inside our church. Lastly, and most difficult of all for me personally, I asked the church to pray with me about the Lord providing $10,000 to provide a way to publish this book.

I was nervous after sensing the Lord calling me to those things and wrestled with the thought that maybe God really was not leading me to do those things at all; that it was me making those things up in my mind because I wanted them so badly. Back and forth I went over and over in my mind wondering if God was really asking me to do those things. I really sensed it was from the Lord and stood before the church asking them to believe with me for all three. I was way, way out on a limb.

I received an email the following Thursday morning with the first of three answers to those specific prayer requests. A lady commented that she had prayed about the family needing a vehicle. Here is what her email said:

> Good morning Matt. Don [not his real name] and I were wondering if the family you talked about Sunday was still in need of a vehicle? Sunday when you asked us to pray about it I prayed that if it were God's will he would also place this desire on Don's heart. When we got home I almost said something to Don but restrained myself and waited. A little while later Don said, "Would you want to donate your van?" I was shocked. I *knew* this was God using us to help another family. The van needed a little work so

we have had it in to [the dealership] this week getting some things fixed. Don got it inspected yesterday so other than running it through the car wash
it is ready to go.

Thanks,

Samantha (not her real name)

It was a real joy to watch them give so sacrificially and so
joyfully to the Lord and that family.

The next Sunday afternoon I had a visitor come to my
office. We talked over several issues when finally my guest
told me they had been extremely blessed at work and had
some money to give to the church and did not know where
to designate it. This faithful servant wanted to know if I had
thoughts about where the money should go. I reminded this
person about our prayer for a new parsonage. The check was
given in the amount of $30,000. Hallelujah! God had hon-
ored two of the three things we prayed about but there was
still the prayer about the publication of my book.

While praying about the book being published I sensed
the Lord asking me to give all the money made from book
sales to the building fund of our church. I committed to that
and about a week later I received this email from our trea-
surer:

Matt: Through April $925 has been donated to pub-
lish your book. I received an anonymous donation of
$9,000 for the printing of the book. This brings the
total to $9, 925. Praise the Lord!

Not an hour later a lady stopped by my office. She
walked in and sat down quickly. She never quit talking and
hurriedly took her checkbook out and wrote two different
checks for $250, the two combined totaling $500. She had

no idea what a role she was playing in a long delayed answer to prayer. Her gifts that same day brought the total to print this book to $10,425. It was just like the miracle of the loaves and the fish—God supplied more than was needed. Once again I was given a front row seat to behold God at work and to demonstrate His power.

Let me conclude this chapter with two more faith stories. Five years ago our television suddenly went on the blink without warning. It was over a decade old. This happened during our extreme faith makeover time, and therefore going out to buy another television was not an option. We were trusting God for tanks of gas, meals, and money to pay our bills. Financing a new television was not an option either. In the whole scheme of things, having another television was way down on our list of priorities. We took the small one from our bedroom and put it in our large entertainment center, where it looked a little silly but was sufficient. We did not make a big deal about it; in fact we never mentioned it and went on with life.

Nobody would have ever known our situation except for the fact that I used that small television to show a video clip one Sunday morning as part of our Bible study. Some good friends asked about our old television, and we told them it had broken and was beyond repair. We had seen God do so many other miracles that trusting Him for a television was not that big of a deal. There were a few prayers lifted concerning it, but like I said, a new television was certainly not a priority or a necessity.

Several days later my friend Mark asked me if I would go with him to help load and unload a new big screen television he was buying. He came by to pick me up, and we drove to Best Buy. Mark made arrangements to get his television, and then he told *me* to pick out a television for my family. I objected, but he insisted and finally picked out a television for us! I protested the whole time, but he was not to be denied the blessing of blessing us. That TV was bigger and nicer than any TV we had owned before, and we knew it was another miracle. God used Mark and Sandy to once again show us His faithfulness, and once again our confidence in the Lord grew. Even today I am humbled that God allowed us to have that television. It still sits in our living room, and we have enjoyed many family movie nights watching it. While writing the conclusion to this chapter, I was sitting in my living room writing on a notepad. The boys and I were watching the Texas Rangers play against the Houston Astros on that very TV that God had given us. I stopped writing long enough to tell the boys the story of how God provided it, because I never want them to forget or to be unaware of God's miraculous power demonstrated in our lives continually.

Psalm 78:5-6 says,

For He established a testimony in Jacob And appointed a law in Israel, Which He has commanded our fathers That they should teach them to their children, That the generation to come might know, even the children yet to be born, That they might arise and tell them to their children.

Brenda and I want the boys to develop confidence in God even at this young age.

During this past Christmas season I asked the boys what they wanted, and was I ever in for a shock. Tanner was the first to speak up—he wanted a trampoline for all of the brothers. Our eldest, Taylor, spoke up next and said he wanted a go-cart. *Whoa*! I realized then that as our boys had grown so had the items that held their fascination, but both trampolines and go-carts were out of our price range as potential Christmas gifts.

I tried not to show my dismay as I reminded them that Jesus was the one who gave us gifts and miracles and that they had better start praying for those gifts. We even stopped and prayed right then. I was amazed then and am still amazed at the confidence of those little boys in asking the Lord for things. They really believe that the Lord hears and responds (much more so than their parents do at times).

Weeks went by, and our sons seldom failed to ask the Lord for the trampoline or the go-cart in prayer. Before Thanksgiving God provided when Brenda and I were given a gift card by some church members that more than paid for the trampoline. The go-cart, however, was another story.

I have to confess that I struggled with even thinking that a go-cart might be in God's will for the boys to have. It is not like they *needed* a go-cart. I went my entire childhood without a motorized toy of any kind. But I prayed about it on and off, and Brenda began researching go-carts on the Internet. We found lots of deals, but, as so often is the case, the Lord did not make provision, and so we were left to wait.

One week before Christmas, I got up early on a Saturday morning and went to my office. When I opened my office door I found a card on the floor, and inside the card I found $200. I immediately went to the Lord and asked if the go-cart was in His will. When I left the office I remembered a gift of some shoes one of our ladies wanted me to drop off for a widower in our church, so I went by his house, gave him the shoes, and visited with him for a few minutes. Reaching for his wallet, he asked me what the boys wanted for Christmas. I told him they didn't need anything (which was the truth), and he pulled out a $100 bill. He insisted on giving it to me to use for the boys, and in the middle of resisting, I was reminded of my prayers about the go-cart. Humbly I accepted his gift and hurried home to tell Brenda.

We looked all over town the following week and found that we really needed about $600 more to get a go-cart. Brenda and I prayed and left the matter in God's hands, but by Christmas Eve the Lord had not made any more provision. I was very sad for Taylor—his faith had grown so much over those weeks. He even began to pray that he only wanted the go-cart if it was God's will, and if not he would understand. I wanted him to have that go-cart, not because he deserved it but so that his faith would be encouraged and strengthened.

Christmas morning came and went with no go-cart, but Taylor never mentioned it. I could see the hurt in his eyes, however, and it reminded me of a similar Christmas when I was a boy and did not get the one thing I wanted most. We still had a great Christmas, though, and enjoyed being together as a family and celebrating the birth of Christ.

The next day I went to the office as usual. A man called me and asked if he could come by to see me. When he arrived he handed me an envelope and told me not to ask any questions. When I opened it, there was a check inside for $3,250. I was dumbfounded.

After he left, I called Brenda and told her to stop whatever she was doing and come to my office. She gathered up all the boys and brought them to the church, and I met them outside and opened that check in front of all of them. At first, they were confused and thought the check was for $300, so I encouraged them to look closer. Taylor understood, and looked at me with hope in his eyes for that go-cart. I told him that God had made that miracle happen for that very reason, and those four little boys all jumped and down and cheered like fans at the Super Bowl.

We went out and looked at go-carts and quickly determined that one that Taylor would fit in would be too big for the other boys. We settled on four-wheelers, and a man from our church made us a great deal so we were able to get *two* four-wheelers rather than one small go-cart.

It was several weeks later when Brenda made a great observation—she said that the Lord had waited to give us those four-wheelers until *after* Christmas so the boys would know that *He* had given them, not a fat jolly man in a red suit. My boys will never forget that miracle.

This chapter has been especially laced with numerous faith stories in order to encourage you. I tell them not to boast in my prayer life but to assure you that anything the Lord has done for my family He can most assuredly do for your family. I hope that these stories will inspire you to have greater confidence in God regardless of what you are facing. May your life of prayer prove out the truth of 1 John 5:14-15 over and over again, so the generations yet to be born will inherit a rich legacy of faith as they too behold God's faithfulness.

CHAPTER 14

God's Glory: The Ultimate End of Prayer

WE HAVE TRAVELED A LONG WAY THROUGH THE PAGES OF this book, and our journey together is nearing an end. Before we part ways, there is one last issue I would like to address: What is the ultimate end of prayer?

The ultimate end of prayer is not just to get a desired answer or to witness a miracle; it is not even to give testimonies about what we have seen. The ultimate end of prayer is for *God* to get *more glory*. With each page, each testimony and each chapter of this book, that has been my desire—to glorify God. The primary focus of our prayer lives should be to make much of Him and little of us.

God desires to bring more and more glory to His name. *"For My own sake, for My own sake, I will act, For how can My name be profaned? And My glory I will not give to another"* (Isa. 48:11). In fact, I would submit to you that there is nothing God is more passionate about than spreading the glory of His name. After reading many books written by John Piper and listening to several of his messages he helped me discover this truth. His fame is utmost on His mind and heart; therefore, what God wants more than anything from our prayers is that He gets the glory for answering them. Put in other words, God wants all the credit. We don't get any, but how we try to hoard the credit and glory for ourselves! We want people to recognize our prayers, our faith, and our persistence, when in reality it is God who graces us with all those things. He does the work, He lifts the burden, He provides for the need, He moves the mountains, and therefore He alone should get the glory.

Too often we exalt the person doing the praying as if by their own ability they produced the answers, but nothing could be farther from the truth. God determines to listen. He could turn a deaf ear, but He chooses to listen and to be attentive to our prayers, as in Psalm 4:1 and Psalm 5:1. God chooses to intervene and meet our needs, as we read in Philippians 4:19. If God does all the work, the logical conclusion is that He should get all the glory.

There are several ways to ensure that the Lord gets all the credit for the answers to your petitions. Psalm 105:1-5 identifies several ways we can do this. First, we can thank Him. *"Oh give thanks to the LORD, call upon His name; Make known His deeds among the peoples"* (Ps. 105:1). What if after reading this you put this book down and spent as much time as you could just giving Him thanks for specific things in your life? What if you took out a notepad and pen and began making a list of all the things you want to thank God for—how long would your list be? How many pages? How many notepads? You could start by thanking Jesus for grace, the free gift of salvation, His Word, preachers and teachers, His guidance and protection, your family, home, vehicle, last meal, the ability to breathe, and the list could go on and on. We spend far too much time whining about what we don't have rather than thanking the Lord for what we have been given.

When you give God thanks, you are intentionally putting all the focus on Him; in essence you are spotlighting the greatness and the faithfulness of God. His glory is spread when this takes place. God loves to be thanked—we all do. I know what a heartfelt "Thank you" means to me.

This past school year, Taylor, Tanner, and Tucker would periodically ask me to have lunch with them at school. One day Taylor asked me to have lunch with him, but it was not a great day for me to do that where my schedule was concerned. He pleaded, so I reluctantly consented, and he made a special request for food from one of his favorite restaurants. Well, things began going south from the very beginning. First, I got tied up at the office and left late, knowing that I had to drive to another town to get Taylor's favorite food. Then the line at the restaurant was longer than normal, leaving me farther behind schedule, so I decided to go through the drive-through to save time. I could not believe it when I arrived at the drive-through speaker and discovered that it was broken. Stuck in the line of cars, I had to wait until I arrived at the window to place my order, which took more time to fill, leaving me farther behind schedule. I finally got our food, and I drove as fast as I dared back to Taylor's school, only to discover that I was even later than I thought because I had the wrong lunchtime in my head in the first place. Taylor had been waiting for me nearly half of his lunch period. Frustrated with the whole situation, I made my way to Taylor, and his teacher graciously allowed the two of us to sit at a table all by ourselves (which I appreciated, since I was in no mood to be around a bunch of fifth graders). But then as Taylor opened up his food and began to munch on burritos and tacos he said something that changed everything: "Dad, thank you for bringing lunch to me. I love this special time we are having together." How did that make me feel? Honored! It was worth all the stress and hassle to bring him lunch. All the strain of that morning melted under the radiant face of a grateful and adoring child. In fact, *I* was blessed for bringing him lunch. If a son's comments can do that do the heart of an earthly father, how must God feel when we get lost in the gratitude of worship? Our thankful expressions can actually bless God and bring even more glory to His name.

When I walked into the cafeteria that day, it made Taylor the envy of every child in his class—not because of me, but because they all wanted his lunch! But Taylor's expression of gratitude made me want to bring him lunch over and over again throughout the course of that year, which I did. In the same way, God longs to bless His children and is pleased when we are grateful for the things He gives us and does for us.

Another way we can bring glory to God is by making His deeds known among the people (Ps. 105:1). As the Lord continually works miracles and moves in our lives, our responsibility is to continually tell His deeds to the people. That is exactly what I have tried do throughout this book. I have highlighted several dramatic answers to prayer so your faith would be encouraged and you would see the glory of God. We should be constantly testifying in our families, at work, at school, in our Bible study groups, in worship services, among the lost, and among even the most seasoned saints. Each time we do this, God receives more glory, which is the whole point of His answering our prayers in the first place. So, do not be tight-lipped about all the Lord does in your life. Let people know, so they can be inspired to believe for themselves, and the glory of the Lord will expand in one home after another, from one community to another, and eventually to all the nations of the world.

Brenda and I have included our boys in many of our prayer concerns. They have prayed right along with us and have seen on more than one occasion that the answer did not come without persevering prayer. After having received a $500 financial blessing a few years ago, we allowed the oldest boys to each hold a $100 bill in their tiny hands as tangible proof of how the Lord had heard and responded to our prayers. I pray that moment was forever etched on their minds and hearts.

I took one of my boys with me when God performed a miracle in giving me a Jeep Grand Cherokee in place of the worn-out truck I was driving at the time. He and I received the keys to that vehicle together and drove it back home. He mentioned that story just the other day while we were together in our living room. I pray that his little heart was forever overwhelmed by the power of God as mine was that night—I can still remember driving that Jeep home, rejoicing in God's faithfulness. I have told that story at camps, retreats, and church revivals in New Mexico, California, Louisiana, Oklahoma, Arkansas, and all over the state of Texas. I *had* to tell people about the great God I serve and what He had done for me. He did the miracle, and He got the glory.

That's the point—we tell the stories, and God gets more and more glory, which in turn encourages greater faith in the hearts of the listeners. Hopeless and desperate people long and need to hear that God has not abandoned them and that He does come through even in the darkest of nights. How will these people be encouraged if we never share what the Lord has done for us publicly? Our mouths must not be sealed but should be unmuzzled to spread His fame.

When was the last time you heard fresh testimonies in a worship service? I have sat through countless services where not one testimony of the power of God was given. I have heard the awkward silence as some leader tries to coax a testimony from the lips of some tight-lipped servant of the Lord. Maybe the reason for the awkward silence is that the majority have chosen to live by sight rather than faith. These people have chosen to depend on themselves or others rather than God. If you are always solving your own problems, you will also be giving yourself the glory. Inevitably, though, a problem will come that you cannot solve; it will be too big for you to lift and too costly for your limited resources. What then? Sooner or later you will have to depend on God or go down in a heap of broken and twisted dreams dashed on the rocks of reality that crush your faith and extinguish hope. A person living without hope is a pathetic sight, and that's why hopeless people must hear about God's deeds in our lives. They must! And when they do, God is glorified and His power is exalted.

Psalm 105:2-3 also tells us that God is glorified through our singing. Just this past Sunday we were singing in church, and the Lord really used one particular song. Its lyrics exalted the sovereignty of God in both the good times and bad times. I sang that song from my front row pew as a prayerful declaration in my own life and over the lives of our congregation. Much of our worship through singing is prayers put to music, or, I should say, it should be. As we pray through our singing, the glory of the Lord flows like a river, sweeping up those who love the Lord and trust Him. God was exalted and glorified in my heart Sunday morning, which helped my preaching and prayerfully cast hope for the many who were suffering and needed a fresh word from the Lord. My heart really connected with God during that song, and God became more real to me; therefore I was able to preach with passion and love for God as opposed to regurgitating a mechanical message from my mind rather than my heart. God is not glorified when this happens.

When we sing with hearts filled with love, passion, and devotion, God is glorified. He is exalted and made more famous in the hearts of people all over the world. This is the whole point of prayer and living as a child of God—to make Him famous. He deserves all the credit, all the acclaim, and all the glory.

How I pray that through our praying, testifying, thanking, and singing, God is exalted and His glory will spread. *"For the earth will be filled With the knowledge of the glory of the LORD, As the waters cover the sea"* (Hab. 2:14). As we continually behold His faithfulness, let us determine that He alone gets the glory.

Conclusion

I SAID IN THE BEGINNING THAT THIS WOULD BE THE MOST ambitious book I have ever attempted to write...and it has been. Over these months of writing and rewriting this manuscript, I have relished the reliving of the multiple times we have witnessed the powerful hand of God at work in our lives and the lives of those closely associated with us. It has been an amazing adventure of faith that has thrilled my soul.

I know these few words and chapters can never exhaust the fullness of the subject of prayer. This has merely been my feeble attempt to encourage desperate people to continue clinging to hope through fire-breathed and faith-filled praying.

The pages of this book have been hammered out in my office, in a private cabin overlooking a picturesque lake, in a rocking chair on the back porch of a vacation resort, and once in a Sunday school class (when I was on vacation). Over the course of writing this book, I have continued to see the good hand of God blessing me. I have been stretched and found God faithful over and over again. I do not write as one lecturing on theory; I have lived out these truths on the anvil of real life and real ministry.

It is my hope that this simple book will do two things. First, I hope it will inspire thousands upon thousands to pray, to believe God for more than they could have ever imagined (Eph. 3:20). Second, I hope that this book will stand the test of time, because the truths of Scripture are timeless. To God alone be the glory for what happens next.